A DESCRIPTION OF THE NEW YORK CENTRAL PARK

TERRACE FROM ROCK IN RAMBLE.

A

DESCRIPTION

OF THE

NEW YORK

CENTRAL PARK

CLARENCE C. COOK

With an Introduction by
MAUREEN MEISTER

WASHINGTON MEWS BOOKS
An Imprint of
NEW YORK UNIVERSITY PRESS
New York

WASHINGTON MEWS BOOKS

An Imprint of

NEW YORK UNIVERSITY PRESS
New York
www.nyupress.org

A Description of the New York Central Park was originally published in 1869
by F. J. Huntington and Co.

ISBN: 978-1-4798 -7746-1

For Library of Congress Cataloging-in-Publication data,
please contact the Library of Congress.

New York University Press books are printed on acid-free paper, and
their binding materials are chosen for strength and durability.
We strive to use environmentally responsible suppliers and
materials to the greatest extent possible
in publishing our books.

Manufactured in the United States of America
10 9 8 7 6 5 4 3 2 1

CONTENTS

INTRODUCTION

"A Work of National Interest": The Book and the Men behind It

MAUREEN MEISTER

If you have picked up this book, you probably know something already about New York City's Central Park. If you have paged through this book, you probably have found yourself seduced by its illustrations. Published in 1869, it features dozens of wood engravings that represent scenes and highlights of the park, designed by Frederick Law Olmsted and Calvert Vaux for the competition they won in 1858. Familiar attractions include the elm-lined Mall, the Bow Bridge, and the Balcony Bridge. At the same time, the modern reader is intrigued by hoop-skirted Victorian women accompanying well-behaved charges, a couple riding in a sleigh, or, on one of the last pages, a shepherd tending tranquil sheep. The reader may be struck by how the park has changed, perhaps noticing that there wasn't always a sculpture in the Bethesda Terrace fountain or that the music stand at the head of the Mall no longer exists. In a similar vein, as the text leads the reader from one area to the next, observations about architectural and natural elements give rise to thoughts about what continues to be the same and what has changed or vanished altogether.

A Description of the New York Central Park, reprinted here, was not the first book to have been issued about this now cherished place. Nevertheless, this is one of the most important books ever to have been produced on the subject, and it continues to be both memorable and authoritative. Its author, Clarence Chatham Cook, is recognized today as one of the nation's earliest and most prominent art critics.

The artist, Albert Fitch Bellows, was a well-regarded painter and illustrator. Less well-known yet also deserving recognition is the publisher, Francis Junius Huntington, who brought the book to fruition. It was he who committed the resources to create a volume of the highest quality, paying for superior engravings, printing, and binding. Huntington also made up his mind that he wouldn't rush the process. Work on the book began in the middle of 1865, and after three and a half long years, it was on the market in December 1868.[1] From the beginning, the book was going to be special in every respect. Who then were its creators and what were the motivations behind its publication?

STRUGGLES OVER THE PARK

Before turning to these questions, we would do well to take stock of how the park and its designers were faring during the mid- to late 1860s. At the time when Bellows was sketching, Cook was writing, and Huntington was lining up the engravers and printer, debates were being waged over the character of the park and proposals that would affect it. Indeed, struggles over the development of the park are integral to its history, having started soon after Olmsted and Vaux won the design competition and construction got under way in 1858.[2] The partners' authority and the status of their employment changed frequently. At first Olmsted was appointed architect-in-chief and Vaux was paid as his assistant, and then Vaux was more formally employed as consulting architect.[3] But by 1861, the Central Park Commission limited the role of the designers, placing Andrew H. Green, the park's comptroller, over them. In June of that year, with the onset of the Civil War, Olmsted left New York for Washington, D.C., to serve as executive secretary of the U.S. Sanitary Commission, established to meet the medical needs of the Union Army, and Vaux carried on under Green. Two years later, an exasperated Vaux submitted his resignation; however, by 1865 he and Olmsted sought to be reinstated, and they were reappointed as landscape architects of the park in July, positioning them to pursue their vision.[4]

Although the basic plan prepared by Olmsted and Vaux was secure, several troublesome issues emerged during the 1860s that demanded attention. At the beginning of 1865, the most disturbing threat to their overall concept was a proposal to erect gateways at the southern end of the park.[5] Designed by the distinguished architect Richard Morris Hunt, who had trained in Paris at the École des Beaux-Arts, they were lavishly sculpted, very much in line with the civic projects being erected in Second Empire France. But Vaux considered the gateways inappropriate for the image that he and Olmsted had developed for an American park, which he believed should welcome visitors without imperial fanfare. The park was to emphasize nature, not architecture. Vaux made his case into a cause, writing a letter in May that was published on the front page of the *New York Evening Post*.[6] Not coincidentally, the paper's editor was William Cullen Bryant, an early champion of a major park for New York City. Two days later, the park board decided to set the matter of the gates aside, but no one could be certain that the debate was over for good.[7]

Another concern for the park's designers was the donation of sculpture, often commemorative, which threatened to intrude upon landscapes that were conceived as retreats into nature.[8] The commissioners shared the view that these monumental gifts were problematic. A third issue was the desire by various groups for programmed spaces. For example, certain city residents wanted to claim the expansive southwestern lawn, called the Green, for military drills, which did not mesh well with the pastoral vision of the landscape architects or the park board. To counter this pressure and preserve the quiet in the contested territory, sheep and a shepherd were installed there around 1864.[9]

FRANCIS JUNIUS HUNTINGTON, PUBLISHER

In the meantime, as the decade progressed, visitors thronged to the park, and publishing a fancy book about it promised to be a smart venture. In September 1865 the firm of Bunce and Huntington announced in a trade magazine that a book called *The Central Park* was "in press."[10] The following March, the magazine reported that the title would come out in May.[11] It would be illustrated by Albert Fitch Bellows "of the National Academy" and "elegantly printed and bound." It also would be sold at a "moderately low price." The announcement was a bit optimistic, although the publishers surely didn't expect that the book would take so long to appear and would cost so much. By the end of 1868, following the dissolution of the partnership between Bunce and Huntington, F. J. Huntington and Company issued a prospectus, offering a book "for the holiday season" now titled *A Description of the New York Central Park*.[12] It would be "a work of national interest" and could be bought as a cloth edition with gilt ornament at ten dollars or bound in morocco leather, "full gilt," at fifteen dollars. To impress potential buyers with the quality of the artwork, three sample pages and four of the 101 wood engravings that had been completed were reproduced. The book would measure 6½ by 9 inches, and it would include two maps, one of the southern end and the other of the northern end of the park, representing "every winding road and minutest footpath." Decorating its front and back covers would be a round emblem with the monograms of the park's designers and the letters *C* and *P* in the center. It had become a luxury product. When perusing lists of books for sale during this period, we find that most books cost between pennies to a little over a dollar, and a well-illustrated book could be purchased for around five dollars.[13]

In July 1866 *Miller's New Guide to Central Park* came out, published by James Miller and written and illustrated by T. Addison Richards.[14] The clothbound book, which included a map, targeted the mainstream market and was priced at $1.25. Richards was an artist of little distinction, and his name would not have been a selling point. He produced seventeen drawings, two engraved and signed by "Richardson," likely James H. Richardson, which were relatively coarse in execution. For the most part, the text was flat, but occasionally the author volunteered an opinion. Richards called Hunt's designs for the southern entrance gates "admirable," and he expressed his hope that they would soon be built.[15] Also in 1866 D. Van Nostrand published a five-dollar book devoted to Hunt's gates, including five colored lithographic views and four plans.[16] Bunce and Huntington envisioned a volume that would reflect entirely different sympathies.

A native New Yorker, Oliver Bell Bunce (1828–1890) was an author and playwright who made his living as an editor and a sometime publisher. During the mid-1860s, he partnered with Huntington, leaving the firm in 1867 to work for the house of D. Appleton and Company, eventually serving as the editor of *Appleton's Journal*.[17] Unlike Bunce, Francis Junius Huntington (1802–1878) found his calling as a publisher. Born in Hartford to a distinguished Connecticut family, he and his brother Hezekiah established a bookstore and began publishing together.[18] For most of his life, Francis lived on an estate in West Hartford, but by the 1830s he had opened a publishing house in New York City. The many atlases and songbooks of religious music that he issued required production skills that would be useful later for an illustrated book on Central Park.

The decision that Bunce and Huntington made in 1865 to offer a book about the park may be explained by another title they released that year. This book was *Soldiers' Letters, from Camp, Battle-field and Prison*, edited by Lydia Minturn Post and published for the U.S. Sanitary Commission, the organization that had been directed by Olmsted to support the Northern Army during the Civil War.[19] The question then is who from the Sanitary Commission established the relationship with Bunce and Huntington? If that person were Olmsted, he was well positioned to propose to the publishers that they develop a book on Central Park. Having just been reinstated by the park board in July, Olmsted and Vaux were eager to promote their original intentions.

Another person who would have encouraged Bunce and Huntington to take on the book was the Reverend Henry W. Bellows, who founded the Sanitary Commission and hired Olmsted to run it. Bellows was the minister of All Souls Unitarian Church, which Vaux and his wife attended.[20] Located at Fourth Avenue and 20th Street and built between 1853 and 1855, it was designed by Jacob Wrey Mould, who later worked with Vaux on the ornament and structures for the park. Bellows was closely aligned with these men, and they socialized together. Both Olmsted and Vaux were members of the Century Association, an art-oriented club on East 15th Street that Henry Bellows had helped establish.[21] In 1861 he wrote a lengthy article in the *Atlantic Monthly* about the new park, commending it as "a royal work, undertaken and achieved by the Democracy."[22] While the park might well be admired as a royal work, it did not originate as royal property as did the major parks of Europe. Bellows appreciated how New York's Central Park developed "both in its creation and growth, in its use and application, new and almost incredible tastes, aptitudes, capacities, and powers in the people themselves." That the park would be used by residents of moderate wealth and the poor also appealed to him. Finally, Bellows responded to specific criticisms of the park, defending decisions such as planting young trees and separating the walks from the carriage roads. As Olmsted and Vaux campaigned for their vision for the park during the mid-1860s, it would have been like Bellows to suggest a book on the topic to the men who were issuing a book for the Sanitary Commission.

By the end of 1865, Bunce and Huntington announced the publication of another volume that prepared them to take on the Central Park book. Called *The Festival of Song: A Series of Evenings with the Poets*, it was heralded as "the great illustrated book of the year" and featured seventy-three original drawings by "the leading artists" of the National Academy of Design.[23] The claim was not an exaggeration. Contributors included many worthies such as Frederic E. Church, Asher B. Durand, and Worthington Whittredge. Albert Fitch Bellows also was commissioned, bringing him into contact with the publishers. The book was available at three prices, the most expensive being a deluxe version at twenty dollars. Bunce and Huntington had landed on an opportunity to cater to a niche market. Years later, Bunce was identified as a "pioneer" in developing a line of books that consisted of "superbly illustrated poems for holiday sale."[24] Clearly pleased with *The Festival of Song*, the partners decided to publish an extensively illustrated volume on Central Park.

Just what snags the men encountered next is not known. But after Bunce left the partnership, Huntington was determined to see the project through and maintain a high standard of production. At this point in his life, he was sufficiently well off to carry the costs, and he would have recognized that he might not recover his investment—and indeed, the project may have been a financial failure. Yet even if he did lose money on it, he would reap social benefits associated with the effort. In the 1860 *Trow's New York City Directory*, Huntington listed his publishing business at 7 Beekman Street and his home in Hartford. By 1865 he was selling books at 434 Broome Street, ran a bindery at 15 Vandewater Street, and listed his home at Gramercy Park. Publishing fine art books enhanced his standing as he reoriented himself to New York City.

CLARENCE CHATHAM COOK, AUTHOR

If Olmsted or Henry Bellows was the first to suggest issuing a book on Central Park to Bunce and Huntington, the publishers would have needed to sign on a sympathetic author. Clarence Chatham Cook (1828–1900) was such an individual. If the idea to publish the book started with Bunce and Huntington, they would have sought out Cook as someone who could deliver an engaging text. Yet another possibility is that Cook proposed the project to the publishers. But when the book appeared, Cook was not identified as the author, which one might expect had he been the force behind the endeavor. In all likelihood, he was tapped once the concept of the book started to take form.

Cook came from New England stock and spent the early years of his childhood in Boston.[25] His father, Zebedee Cook Jr., was a founder of the Massachusetts Horticultural Society, and a love of nature would be shared by father and son. When Clarence was ten, the family moved to New York City.[26] He later recalled, "My first sight of New York astonished me. Such noise, such bustle, such dirt, such crowds of wallowing pigs! It was long before I became used to such barbarisms and I hate them as heartily now as I did then."[27] After several attempts to settle a miserable Clarence in local schools, the father escorted him to a boarding school in Tarrytown to prepare for college. The educational experience was an unhappy one, but Clarence found his passion in the meadows of the region along the Hudson River. From there he returned to the Boston area, entering Harvard and graduating with the class of 1849. During his senior year he enrolled as a special student in the Lawrence Scientific School, where he studied zoology, and he served as the class artist.[28] By early 1852, Cook was back in the Hudson River valley, working in Newburgh, New York, for Andrew Jackson Downing, the renowned landscape gardener and author, and his partner, Calvert Vaux.[29] Downing had been writing about the desirability of large parks for the nation's urban centers and specifically a major park for New York City, ideas that made a lasting impression on the young assistant. When Cook drafted his manuscript for the book on Central Park, he would remind readers about Downing's advocacy. Also Cook met a sister of Downing's wife during this period, and they wed in October 1852.

The couple settled in New York City, and Cook embarked on a writing career. He focused on art criticism, contributing as a staff writer to a weekly called the *Independent*. Yet he was interested in all fields that involved design. In a column from 1855, he asserted that New Yorkers needed "a Park, and a great one, to serve higher ends."[30] Cook also wrote for *Putnam's Monthly*, one of whose owners and editors was Olmsted. Cook had a renegade streak, and by the early 1860s he had joined a like-minded group of artists, architects, and artistic types who embraced the views of the English critic John Ruskin.[31] In 1863 they founded the Association for the Advancement of Truth in Art, promoting Gothic Revival architecture and paintings that were executed with painstaking attention to natural detail. Cook also led the members in launching a journal, the *New Path*, editing it during its first year from his home on East 29th Street. Except for the first three issues, the *New Path* was published by James Miller—the same James Miller who would publish *Miller's New Guide to Central Park* in 1866 by T. Addison Richards.[32] When the Miller guidebook came out, Cook must have been well aware of it. And given his high artistic standards, he wouldn't have thought much of Richards as either an author or an artist. Cook would have recognized the potential for a book that was better written and illustrated.

In 1864 Cook was hired as a staff member and art critic for the *New-York Daily Tribune*, Horace Greeley's respected newspaper. The appointment was a plum position, and he established himself as one of the most influential voices in the history of American art criticism. Cook became known for his sharp judgments, as someone who didn't hesitate to upbraid even the leading artists of his time. But he also encouraged support for the nation's artists, and he wrote with humor and intelligence. He felt strongly about his independence as a writer. In a letter to Henry Bellows, written in 1866 on *Tribune* letterhead, Cook explained why he was returning money that Bellows had sent with a book he had hoped to promote.[33] Cook apologized profusely to the minister, not wishing to insult him for any wrongdoing, while telling him that the *Tribune* "strives after impartiality." Perhaps due to the same desire for detachment from the artists he discussed in his reviews, Cook never joined the Century Association.

In early August 1865, Cook devoted a column in the *Tribune* to Hunt's designs for the Central Park gates.[34] Cook referred explicitly to the "excellent letter" by Vaux that had run in the May issue of the *New York Evening Post*. Many more of Cook's points drew upon a fourteen-page letter that Vaux sent to him in June.[35] Cook's concept of independence as a writer apparently didn't apply to the subject of the park and his interactions with its designers. He and the landscape architects were allies. As usual, Cook's *Tribune* article was unsigned, but the sharp words were distinctively his. The gates by Hunt, he declared, were "both ugly and unsuitable." Cook told his readers that Central Park was American, with a plan "founded on the purest and most elevated democratic ideas." It was unlike the English parks, with "wild tracts of grass and trees," and it was unlike the French and other European parks, with their artificiality. The park's designers, Cook explained, believed "that everything in our social and political life exists by and for the people," rejecting class interests, "because there are no fixed classes." Returning to the subject of Hunt's gates, Cook derided them as "the barren spawn of French Imperialism." He elaborated, "We don't like to be reminded of the existence of such riff-raff as the French Emperor, when we are in our Park." But the heart of the matter for Cook was the priority Vaux and Olmsted had placed on minimizing the role of architecture in the park, the one exception being the Terrace. They had developed their plan to emphasize nature over art.

A month later, Bunce and Huntington announced that their book on Central Park was in press, and Cook probably had agreed to write the text by then. If he started a draft right away, he revised it substantially in 1868, or else he wrote it entirely in 1868, when publication was in the offing.[36] After he finished, Cook sent a portion or all of the manuscript to Olmsted, asking him to report on "exactly" what passed through his mind when reading it.[37] In light of the fact that Cook had based much of his *Tribune* article about the park on a letter from Vaux, we may wonder why Cook sent the final draft to Olmsted. Most likely Cook did so because Vaux was away, traveling in Europe from late August and through the fall.[38] In the end, both park designers were afforded opportunities to convey their ideas through Cook's manuscript—a distinction of the Central Park book.

As an organizing conceit, Cook wrote his text as if he were accompanying the reader on an "imaginary visit."[39] Taking us from the southern to the northern regions of the park, looping from east to west and south again, he adopts a colloquial tone, occasionally veering into commentary. For the most part, however, the book is descriptive, as the title suggests. Cook is attentive to the park's manmade components as well as its trees, plants, and birds. On one occasion, he ruminates about the ways development in Manhattan might best proceed, both around and beyond the boundaries of the park.[40]

What may not be obvious to most modern readers are the political intentions in Cook's writing. He frequently alludes to the goals of Olmsted and Vaux, and he acknowledges their contributions. He also recognizes the talents of Mould, and he makes a point of crediting him with specific designs such as the music stand and the masts carrying the banners on the Terrace.[41] Portraits of all three men further emphasize their importance to the creation of the park, and Cook may have proposed the idea of including them. Somewhat surprising are Cook's appreciative words about Green, the park's comptroller, who was often at odds with the landscape architects.[42] These generous comments may have been calculated to keep Green happy.

Cook also addresses specific threats to the park. By 1868 the most exasperating development was the increasing number of commemorative monuments and sculptures being offered to the board. One issue was the questionable artistic quality of the donations. Cook singled out John Quincy Adams Ward as someone whose talents he recognized, but he believed that few other artists were capable of executing first-rate statues.[43] Cook urged people to hold off on these commissions, "for a second-rate statue is like a tolerable egg—it is not to be endured."[44] Another concern of his was the installation of sculptures that might prompt disturbing thoughts among the park's visitors. The *Tigress*, clenching a dead bird in her maw, was an example—a potentially stress-inducing image of carnage in a sylvan setting.[45] But whatever the subject, Cook was not eager to see the park overwhelmed by multiplying statues. He urged the commissioners to respect the natural character of the park and limit the incursion of "artificial objects."[46]

When Cook was finishing his manuscript, the brouhaha over Hunt's French gates had quieted down. The boundary wall was not com-

pletely built, however, and Cook was sensitive to the possibility that
boosters of the gates could revive the proposal. Cook therefore took
the opportunity to explain to his readers why the gates would be out
of keeping with the rest of the park.[47] Another concern was less black-
and-white. Near the end of the book, Cook pondered the difficulty of
balancing the interest of park visitors who wanted to enjoy open lawns
with the interest of others, especially children, to use the lawns for athletic games—two groups with equally reasonable wishes.[48] This balance could be achieved by careful management, and he believed that
the challenge was being handled well.

Throughout his text, Cook supports the basic principles that guided
the designers of the park—principles that had been articulated to him
by Vaux.[49] The aim to prioritize nature over everything else is repeat-
edly stated. At the same time, Cook explains that in pursuing this ob-
jective, Olmsted and Vaux did not leave the park in its natural state.
Instead they designed improvements that were natural in effect, and
once the work was completed, nature would take over. Another principle that runs through the book is the idea that the park was to be a
place where people of all classes would be welcome. In one passage,
Cook asks us to imagine a physician, students, and a washerwoman
crossing the park from one side of the city to the other.[50] By presenting
examples, he avoids preaching to make his points.

In the book's final section, Cook urges his readers to view the park
as evidence of the great potential of republican government.[51] He expresses the same idea in his preface, lauding the park as "proof" of
the good works that government can accomplish while condemning
the "disgraceful" situation in New York City.[52] By this time, Tammany
Hall had become entrenched in virtually every branch of the government.[53] Originally a fraternal society, it had evolved into a powerful
political machine that called the shots in the Democratic Party. Voting
fraud and graft were rampant, masterminded by Tammany leaders. In
1865 the Union League Club, founded by Henry Bellows and Olmsted
among others, appointed a committee to encourage reform in both

local and state government, and a year later, the group was charged with investigating "official corruption in the City."[54] Club members now included Vaux and the *Tribune*'s Greeley, to be joined by Albert Fitch Bellows in 1868.[55] Cook must have been hearing plenty about the pernicious state of affairs. Yet not until 1871 was the plundering of the city coffers exposed, involving millions of dollars pocketed by William "Boss" Tweed and his Tammany associates. In 1868 Cook couldn't have known how pervasive the corruption in New York City had become. Nevertheless, his respect for the management of Central Park would not have been undermined by the later revelations.

Indeed, building Central Park was not just a success for New York City. It had become an achievement of national interest. What Cook didn't write was this: In the aftermath of the Civil War, with the memory of the assassination of Abraham Lincoln still fresh, the park represented an affirmation of American democracy and hope for a united country's future. The construction of the park must be understood in this context.

ALBERT FITCH BELLOWS, ARTIST

From a marketing perspective, it would be fair to say that the main attraction of Bunce and Huntington's book was the artwork by Albert Fitch Bellows (1829–1883). In his publisher's note, Huntington explains that Bellows, "one of our most popular artists," spent many months on his drawings. The volume was designed as a "pleasure-book" rather than a guide. Lots of pictures, beautifully engraved, were to be enjoyed by the reader while relaxing indoors rather than glimpsed while hiking through the Ramble. When we notice Cook's regular references to specific cuts, we realize that the illustrations came first, finished before the manuscript was written.

Considering that the artist was so important to their project, why did Bunce and Huntington choose Bellows? The answer may be simply that after working with him on *The Festival of Song*, they found him to be agreeable and reliable. It's also possible that Henry Bellows promoted him. The men were distant cousins.[56] What's more—and maybe more importantly—they knew each other as fellow members of the National Academy of Design and the Century. Henry joined the National Academy as an honorary member in 1849, and Albert was elected an Academician in 1861. In February 1865, Albert Fitch Bellows became a Centurion. When frequenting the clubhouse, he also could have been sharing cigars and drinks with Olmsted and Vaux, both admitted in 1859, and they may have recommended him to the publishers. Yet another person who might have suggested Bellows for the illustration job was the artist Frederic Church. Church had sponsored Bellows for the Century, and he was friends with Vaux as well. In 1870 Church and Vaux would collaborate on the design and construction of Church's estate, Olana, in Hudson, New York.[57] Church cared about Central Park, too. In November 1871, he was appointed to the city's Department of Public Parks, and he worked with Vaux on a report about a policy for accepting sculpture.[58] Although less likely, one other person who might have recommended Bellows to the publishers was Cook. Cook was related by marriage to the artist Christopher P. Cranch, who participated with Bellows during the 1860s in an effort to popularize watercolor painting.[59] The connections among these men were many. With this understanding, we may interpret the book on Central Park as the reflection of a network of like-minded individuals with overlapping goals for themselves, New York City, and the country.

Bellows was from Boston, and he trained and practiced as an architect.[60] In 1853 he built a Downing-inspired house at the edge of a pond in the commuter suburb of Winchester. Around the same time, he decided to pursue his dream of becoming an artist and began to paint. Two years later, he left for Europe and enrolled in the Royal Academy of Antwerp. His choice was unconventional and distinguished him as the only American studying art in the Low Countries during this period.[61] When he returned to the United States, he settled in New

York City and by 1857 had opened a studio in Dodsworth's Building at 806 Broadway.[62] Working mainly in oils, he combined his interests in genre and landscape painting, reinforced by his expertise in Flemish and Dutch art. By the beginning of the 1860s, his brushwork had become relatively loose. Dabs of color might represent a small figure, and dabs of white could create a glinting effect in a scene with water. At no point did Bellows show any interest in adopting the tight, detailed nature studies favored by the New York Ruskinians, including Cook. As Cook's enthusiasm for the group began to fade, the fact that Bellows had never been an adherent may have struck Cook as a virtue. Although we don't know whether Cook had a vote in the selection of Bellows for the Central Park book, we may be confident that he was comfortable writing a manuscript that would appear with illustrations by this particular artist.

Thanks to the delay in publication, Bellows was able to draw many of the major features that Olmsted and Vaux conceived for the park. By 1868 the Mall, Terrace, and Bow Bridge were completed. But one highlight had just been designed by Vaux: the Belvedere. Working from the architect's drawings, Bellows drew it in finished form, including a western pavilion that would not be built.[63] His early experience as an architect, especially in architectural rendering, would have come in handy. Some of Bellows's most compelling illustrations are miniature versions of the subjects that he favored in his paintings—broad landscape vistas with scudding clouds and images of people in routine activities. He also was attentive to different kinds of trees, representing elms, willows, and oaks. Many of his subjects are reminiscent of seventeenth-century Netherlandish paintings such as scenes of skaters on frozen water and a laborer mowing a park lawn. Bellows never chose to illustrate raucous behavior, whether in his paintings or the park illustrations. He also did not show New York's ostentatious rich in their finery and extravagant carriages, nor did he sketch the city's tattered poor. Bellows framed Central Park as a place of middle-class serenity.

CORYDON ALEXIS ALVORD, PRINTER

In his note to the reader, Huntington gives credit for the book's beautiful printing to "Alvord," implying that this name would be familiar to prospective buyers. Like Huntington, Corydon Alexis Alvord (1813–1874) was a native of Connecticut. In fact, when the Central Park book came out, the men had become neighbors in West Hartford, living just two doors away from each other.[64] Alvord was the classic self-made man. He started out in life as a printer's apprentice in Hartford and then advanced to a role as the foreman of a printing house.[65] In 1845 he started working in New York City, moving around until he landed in a shop at 15 Vandewater Street, where Huntington operated his bindery. Alvord's was known as a special operation where one could bring unusual requests. Old styles of type, ancient and oriental letters—all could be provided. But Alvord could meet modern demands, too.

One of the attractive qualities of Huntington's Central Park book is the way the text occasionally wraps around the engravings. This involved sensitively integrating the lines of type with the blocks for the illustrations. They were cut by the company of Kingdon and Boyd, who signed their names on several images.[66] The way the engravers captured light and shadow as well as so much minute detail encourages the reader to pick up the book and examine the illustrations again and again. Because of the necessary up-front investment, we may assume that Huntington rather than Alvord hired the engravers. Huntington probably knew them fairly well. In an 1868–1869 business directory, Charles D. Kingdon and Matthew T. Boyd listed their partnership as located at 7 Beekman Street, the same address that Huntington listed for his publishing office at the beginning of the decade.[67]

GEOGRAPHY BEHIND THE BOOK

Once we become acquainted with the individuals behind *A Description of the New York Central Park*, we realize that a web of professional and social relationships bound them together. We also realize that these men were bound by shared experiences with certain geographic locations, places that could be considered the geography behind the book. For the most part, the businessmen worked in the neighborhoods near New York City Hall. Vandewater Street, which no longer exists, was southeast of the municipal building, and Beekman Street is in the same area. In 1868 Olmsted, Vaux, and Company listed their office at 110 Broadway, a few blocks to the southwest.[68] When Huntington moved to Broome Street, just north of Canal Street, he was heading away from the older established neighborhoods for downtown businesses. But this address was still well to the south of the favored residential areas.

At the end of the workday, these men went home to streets in the teens through the twenties. Here is where one could find Albert Fitch Bellows, Cook, Vaux, and Bunce.[69] The streets around Gramercy Park, an exclusive private square between East 20th and East 21st, were where Henry Bellows and Huntington resided. For these men, the places where they were most likely to encounter each other included the Century at East 15th Street and the new National Academy of Design building, at Fourth Avenue and 23rd Street, which opened in 1865. What is noteworthy is that none of them lived or worked anywhere near the new Central Park. Committed as they were to it, it was far removed from their everyday activities.

Certain rural areas beyond Manhattan also connected the men to each other, and an appreciation of these places would have cemented their relationships. Staten Island was a ferry ride away from the city, and it began to attract New Yorkers who wanted to retreat to more natural environs. Cook and his wife rented there in the summers during the mid-1860s, and Olmsted and his family moved to the island in 1866.[70] To the north, Newburgh provided shared memories of Downing's home and office for Vaux and Cook. Across the Hudson River and to the east, Fishkill Landing appealed to Cook, who lived there during the early 1850s and later when he retired.[71]

But even more telling were the affinities these men must have felt to each other through their ties to New England, specifically Boston and Hartford. Cook and Albert Fitch Bellows not only remembered Boston from childhood; they both would have returned there to visit family. Cook refers to Boston in his text on Central Park, and Bellows relocated to Boston during the early 1870s.[72] Henry Bellows was another Boston transplant to New York City, and his Unitarian church, All Souls, attracted New Englanders as members. Memories of Hartford were shared by Olmsted and Huntington, who both came from large families that continued to live there. The printer Alvord, a native of Connecticut, was clearly content with his life in Hartford, as demonstrated by his purchase of the property in West Hartford near the Huntington estate. Frederic Church was yet one more individual in this circle who came from Hartford.

With their roots in New England, these men were tethered to New England values. In projects relating to design, they preferred understated, less showy approaches.[73] Those who were reared in Unitarian or Congregationalist households were steeped in a tradition of meetinghouses, and in their encounters with local government, they recalled town meetings. All of this translated into a commitment to a Central Park that was natural rather than formal, and in design that emphasized landscape over architecture. It meant that they believed in the democratic process and were devoted to it. These ideas would have been shared in discussions about the park, and they underpin the values that Cook expresses in the book.

AFTER PUBLICATION

When it was finally released, the book was well received. The *New York Times* reviewer admired its "exquisite" wood engravings, the way it was "elegantly" printed, and the author's "accuracy of detail."[74] It was sold in England, too. A writer in the *Saturday Review* of London commented favorably on the "copious" illustrations and echoed the *Times* reviewer by choosing the word "elegant" to describe the volume.[75]

In the years that followed, Cook published several more articles on Central Park. An 1869 article by him in *Putnam's* addressed the "madness" of all the statuary that was being presented to the park. Cook urged the commissioners to protect it from "such travesties as the Bust of Schiller."[76] In 1873 he devoted a column in the *Tribune* to the new fountain sculpture, the angel by Emma Stebbins.[77] He didn't think it was especially original, but he thought it was tasteful enough—unlike the statues of Morse and Scott. Those two, he wrote, were "exasperating reminders of human incompetence." Later that year, Central Park was the subject of two more articles by Cook that appeared in *Scribner's Monthly*.[78] In the October issue, he continued to vent about the sculpture, objecting to "such an abortion as the Scott," while commenting positively about the sculptures by Ward and Stebbins.[79]

Over time Cook became well-known as the influential art critic for the *Tribune*, remaining in the position until 1883. His diatribes were routine, and few were spared his tough judgments, including Bellows. Cook wanted to see artists develop, whereas he believed that Bellows was guilty of repeating himself. Bellows was in good company, however, with Louis Tiffany, Samuel Colman, and Jasper Cropsey, all of whom Cook criticized for the same offense.[80] Cook went on to publish other books, including *The House Beautiful*, a highly successful volume on interior design from 1877, and *Art and Artists of Our Time* from 1888.[81] When he died, obituaries would credit him with writing the book on Central Park.[82]

The illustrations by Bellows were published on several more occasions. In the September 1873 article that Cook wrote for *Scribner's*, twenty-one of the park drawings and the portraits of Olmsted, Vaux, and Mould appeared. In the October issue, twenty-three of the drawings were published. These Cook liked. Bellows, he observed, "has not made his pictures half as pretty as he might have done and yet said only what was true. We don't think he has dressed up anything in the Park except the Shepherd, and we are glad he did that, for the Shepherd needed it."[83] Some of the book's engravings would appear in at least two other books.[84] Bellows would not pursue illustration, however. He continued to paint in oils while devoting more and more of his time to painting in watercolors, gaining recognition for his output in that medium. He also participated in the etching revival.

In 1869 Huntington's career was drawing to a close. More than twenty-five years older than Cook and Bellows, he was in his late sixties when the book appeared. He would publish few works after that, and he surely considered the Central Park book his crowning achievement.

THE "REMEDY IN OUR HANDS"

In a period of ever-increasing public affection for the park's historic features and public interest in knowing more about its lost elements, Bellows's illustrations continue to be a major attraction of the book. In modern times, accompanying the effort to restore and maintain the park, the Bellows engravings have been reproduced by advocates including Henry Hope Reed and Sophia Duckworth in *Central Park: A History and Guide*, from 1967, and M. M. Graff in *The Men Who Made Central Park* from 1982.[85] Cook's descriptions have proved to be informative and his observations thought-provoking. Graff appreciated Cook's "burning scorn of anything shoddy or second-rate."

Like the park, the book was the creation of a network of men who gravitated to each other in mid-nineteenth-century New York City. The men who contributed to the book—including the publisher, author, and artist, along with the park's designers and supporters—had a range of motivations behind what finally was produced. But as a group, whether building a park or publishing a book, all of them were committed to meeting the highest possible standard for the task at hand. Driven and dedicated, sympathetic in their thinking, they held great hopes for their city and country. Cook captured this broader view when he wrote, "When we are brought to shame by the vile and dishonest government of the City of New York, and reproached with that dishonor as if it were an argument against Republicanism, we point to the perfect order and quiet of the Central Park as a proof that we have the remedy in our hands when we choose to apply it."[86] The park was a validation of America's potential. But if the park were to be a model for the nation, it needed to be promoted in some way. A book, well-illustrated and well-written, "a work of national interest," would be the vehicle to showcase the achievement that was the New York Central Park.

NOTES

1 *American Literary Gazette and Publishers' Circular*, Sept. 1, 1865, p. 196; and *American Literary Gazette and Publishers' Circular*, Jan. 1, 1869, p. 140. A *New York Times* review of Dec. 22, 1868, "The Holiday Books," makes clear that the book was available for the 1868 Christmas market even though the title page gives a publication date of 1869.

2 The history of the park, including debates over its development, has been recounted by many authors. See Henry Hope Reed and Sophia Duckworth, *Central Park: A History and a Guide* (New York: Clarkson N. Potter, 1967); Roy Rosenzweig and Elizabeth Blackmar, *The Park and the People: A History of Central Park* (New York: Cornell University Press, 1992); and Morrison H. Heckscher, *Creating Central Park* (New York: Metropolitan Museum of Art, 2011; reprint of *The Metropolitan Museum of Art Bulletin*, winter 2008).

3 Rosenzweig and Blackmar, *The Park and the People*, pp. 121–22.

4 Ibid., pp. 190–200, 239.

5 See illustrations in Heckscher, *Creating Central Park*, pp. 62–64.

6 Calvert Vaux, letter, *New York Evening Post*, May 9, 1865, p. 1.

7 The park board voted on May 11, 1865. See [Clarence C. Cook], *A Description of the New York Central Park* (New York: F. J. Huntington, 1869), p. 157.

8 Heckscher, *Creating Central Park*, pp. 68–69.

9 Rosenzweig and Blackmar, *The Park and the People*, p. 252.

10 *American Literary Gazette and Publishers' Circular*, Sept. 1, 1865, p. 196.

11 "Notes on Books and Booksellers," *American Literary Gazette and Publishers' Circular*, March 1, 1866, p. 249.

12 "For the Holiday Season," Patricia D. Klingenstein Library, New-York Historical Society, SY1869, no. 7.

13 In the list of new releases in the Jan. 1, 1869, *American Literary Gazette and Publishers' Circular*, p. 140, *A Description of the New York Central Park* is the most expensive book announced.

14 T. Addison Richards, *Miller's New Guide to Central Park* (New York: James Miller, 1866). Publication was announced in *American Literary Gazette and Publishers' Circular*, July 2, 1866, p. 111. The same publisher issued *Miller's New York as It Is* in 1859 and *Miller's New Guide to the Hudson River* in 1866.

15 Richards, *Miller's New Guide to Central Park*, p. 96.

16 Richard M. Hunt, *Designs for the Gateways to the Southern Entrances of the Central Park* (New York: D. Van Nostrand, 1866). The price was listed in the *American Literary Gazette and Publishers' Circular*, June 15, 1866, p. 91. Other relevant publications were Fred B. Perkins, *The Central Park: Photographed by W. H. Guild Jr.* (New York: Carleton, 1864), with photos, descriptions, and a short history; and *Baldwin's Handbook of Central Park*, bound in paper and selling for twenty-five cents, according to the *American Literary Gazette and Publishers' Circular*, Oct. 1, 1866, p. 254.

17 "Oliver Bell Bunce," *Literary World*, June 7, 1890, p. 192.

18 *The Huntington Family in America: A Genealogical Memoir of the Known Descendants of Simon Huntington* (Hartford: Huntington Family Association, 1915), p. 412. See also listings for the Huntingtons in the 1845 *Geer's Hartford City Directory*.

19 Lydia Minturn Post, ed., *Soldiers' Letters, from Camp, Battle-field and Prison* (New York: Bunce and Huntington, 1865).

20 Francis R. Kowsky, *Country, Park, and City: The Architecture and Life of Calvert Vaux* (New York: Oxford University Press, 1998), p. 138.

21 The Century Association was founded in 1847. Information about the members was provided by Timothy J. DeWerff, Century Association Archives.

22 Henry W. Bellows, "Cities and Parks: With Special Reference to the New York Central Park," *Atlantic Monthly*, vol. 7 (April 1861), pp. 428–29.

23 *The Festival of Song: A Series of Evenings with the Poets* (New York: Bunce and Huntington, 1866). See advertisements in *Round Table*, Nov. 18, 1865, p. 173; and Dec. 23, 1865, p. 264.

24 "Oliver Bell Bunce."

25 See entry on Clarence Chatham Cook, *National Cyclopaedia of American Biography*, vol. 10 (New York: James T. White, 1909), p. 167. No monograph has been published on Cook, but he has been the subject of several dissertations, notably the fine work by Jo Ann W. Weiss, "Clarence Cook: His Critical Writings" (Ph.D. diss., Johns Hopkins University, 1976).

26 1849 Class Book, Harvard University Archives, Cambridge, MA, HUD 249.714f, pp. 161–66.

27 Ibid., p. 162.

28 "Clarence Cook," Harvard University Archives, HUG 300.

29 Cook entry, *National Cyclopaedia*; Weiss, "Clarence Cook," pp. 7–8; Kowsky, *Country, Park, and City*, p. 43.

30 Clarence Cook, "The Fine Arts," *Independent*, May 17, 1855, p. 1.

31 Linda S. Ferber and William H. Gerdts, eds., *The New Path: Ruskin and the American Pre-Raphaelites*, exhibition catalog (New York: Brooklyn Museum, 1985).

32   Miller's role is noted only once, in the May 1864 issue of the *New Path*, where it states
     that it was published by him, "with the exception of the first three numbers." See also
     the ad for the *New Path* in the *New York Evening Post*, May 15, 1865, identifying James
     Miller as publisher.

33   Clarence Cook to Henry W. Bellows, Nov. 27, 1866, Massachusetts Historical Society,
     Boston, Ms. N-1829.

34   [Clarence Cook], "Mr. Hunt's Designs for the Gates of the Central Park," *New-York Daily
     Tribune*, Aug. 2, 1865, p. 8.

35   Calvert Vaux to Clarence Cook, June 6, 1865, container 36 (also microfilm reel 32),
     Frederick Law Olmsted Papers, Manuscript Division, Library of Congress, Washington,
     D.C.

36   The fact that Cook was writing or revising his manuscript in 1868 is reflected by his
     references to reports that ran through 1867. See *Description*, pp. 30, 64, 167.

37   Clarence Cook to Frederick Law Olmsted, n.d., container 11 (also microfilm reel 11),
     Olmsted Papers. See also a related letter from Cook to Olmsted, dated "Wednesday 1868."

38   Kowsky, *Country, Park, and City*, p. 198.

39   [Cook], *Description*, p. 42.

40   Ibid., pp. 91–96.

41   Ibid., pp. 45, 56.

42   Ibid., pp. 54–55, 195–96.

43   Ibid., pp. 37, 48.

44   Ibid., p. 48.

45   Ibid., pp. 73–74.

46   Ibid., pp. 79–80.

47   Ibid., pp. 155–59.

48   Ibid., pp. 196–98.

49   Cook develops ideas presented by Vaux in his letter to Cook sent June 6, 1865. Cook also
     in *Description*, pp. 110–11, refers to a comment made by Horace Greeley, which Cook
     would have known about only through Vaux.

50   [Cook], *Description*, p. 41.

51   Ibid., p. 204.

52   Ibid., "Author's Preface."

53   See Jerome Mushkat, *The Reconstruction of the New York Democracy, 1861–1874*
     (Rutherford, NJ: Fairleigh Dickinson University Press, 1981); Kenneth D. Ackerman, *Boss
     Tweed: The Rise and Fall of the Corrupt Pol Who Conceived the Soul of Modern New York* (New
     York: Carroll and Graf, 2005); and Edwin G. Burrows and Mike Wallace, *Gotham: A History
     of New York City to 1898* (New York: Oxford University Press, 1999), pp. 917–31, 1008–12.

54   Henry W. Bellows, *Historical Sketch of the Union League Club* (New York, 1879), pp. 85, 91.

55   Steele W. Hearne, librarian of the Union League Club, provided dates when members
     were admitted. The club was founded in 1863, and Vaux became a member that year.
     Greeley became a member in 1865.

56 Thomas Bellows Peck, *The Bellows Genealogy* (Keene, NH: Sentinel Printing, 1898).

57 Kowsky, *Country, Park, and City*, pp. 206–15.

58 [Clarence Cook], "Central Park: II," *Scribner's Monthly*, vol. 6, no. 6 (Oct. 1873), p. 676.

59 Bellows was the lead author and Cranch a contributor to *Water-Color Painting: Some Facts and Authorities in Relation to Its Durability* (New York: American Society of Painters in Water-Colors, 1868).

60 For an overview of the artist's career, see Maureen Meister, "Expressions of Quiet: The Art of Albert Fitch Bellows," *Magazine Antiques*, Nov.–Dec. 2015, pp. 116–23. See also S. G. W. Benjamin, "Albert F. Bellows," in *Our American Artists* (Boston: D. Lothrop, 1879).

61 Benjamin, "Albert F. Bellows," n.p.

62 Reported in "Sketchings: Domestic Art Gossip," *Crayon*, vol. 4 (Feb. 1857), p. 54.

63 Kowsky, *Country, Park, and City*, pp. 192–94.

64 See map of West Hartford in *Atlas of Hartford City and County* (Hartford, CT: Baker and Tilden, 1869).

65 See *American Dictionary of Printing and Bookmaking* (New York: Howard Lockwood, 1894), p. 17; and Marcus A. Casey, "A Typographical Galaxy," *Connecticut Quarterly*, vol. 2, no. 1 (Jan.–March 1896), pp. 33–34. See also Caryn Hannan, *Connecticut Biographical Dictionary*, vol. 1 (Hamburg, MI: State History Publications, 2008), pp. 22–23.

66 Cuts are signed "Kingdon & Boyd" on pp. 97, 126, 147, 173.

67 Huntington lists his address as 7 Beekman in *Trow's New York City Directory* for 1860; Kingdon and Boyd list the same address for their business in *Wilson's New York City Copartnership Directory* for 1868.

68 See *Wilson's New York City Copartnership Directory* for 1868.

69 City directories are the main source for tracing addresses. See also Kowsky, *Country, Park, and City*, pp. 161, 343 n. 50; and Weiss, "Clarence Cook," pp. 38, 247 n. 20.

70 On Cook, see Linda S. Ferber, "'Determined Realists,'" in Ferber and Gerdts, *The New Path*, p. 23, who cites correspondence from Cook written from Staten Island; on Olmsted, see Charles E. Beveridge, series ed., *Papers of Frederick Law Olmsted*, vol. 8 (Baltimore: Johns Hopkins University Press, 2013), p. 302 n. 2.

71 "Clarence Cook Dead," *New York Times*, June 3, 1900.

72 See Benjamin, "Albert F. Bellows," n.p.

73 Rosenzweig and Blackmar write that the pastoral vision of the park "may have resonated with New Yorkers of New England stock." *The Park and the People*, p. 110.

74 "The Holiday Books."

75 "American Literature," *Saturday Review* (London), Feb. 27, 1869.

76 Clarence Cook, "Table Talk: Central Park Statues," *Putnam's Magazine*, vol. 13, no. 17 (May 1869), p. 641.

77 [Clarence Cook], "Art: Miss Stebbins's Fountain at the Central Park," *New-York Daily Tribune*, May 19, 1873, p. 5.

78 [Clarence Cook], "Central Park," *Scribner's Monthly*, vol. 6, no. 5 (Sept. 1873), pp. 523–39; [Cook], "Central Park II," pp. 673–91.

79 [Cook], "Central Park II," p. 675.

80 C.C., "The Water Color Society," *New-York Daily Tribune*, Feb. 15, 1879, p. 5.

81 Clarence Cook, *The House Beautiful: Essays on Beds and Tables, Stools and Candlesticks* (New York: Scribner, Armstrong, 1877); Clarence Cook, *Art and Artists of Our Time*, 3 vols. (New York: Selmar Hess, 1888).

82 Several obituaries are filed in "Clarence Cook," Harvard University Archives, HUG 300.

83 [Cook], "Central Park II," p. 678.

84 Alfred Tennyson, *Song of the Brook* (Boston: Estes and Lauriat, 1888); Walter Montgomery, ed., *American Art and American Art Collections: Essays on Artistic Subjects by the Best Authors* (Boston: E. W. Walker, 1889), vol. 2, pp. 913–23.

85 Reed and Duckworth, *Central Park*; M. M. Graff, *The Men Who Made Central Park* (New York: Greensward Foundation, 1982). A facsimile reprint of the book was issued by Benjamin Blom of New York in 1972 and 1979, but it did not include an introduction or other commentary.

86 [Cook], *Description*, p. 204.

THE CENTRAL PARK.

VIEW, LOOKING NORTH, NEAR MUSEUM.

A

DESCRIPTION

OF THE

NEW YORK

CENTRAL PARK.

PUBLISHER'S NOTE.

It is hoped that this work will please the public to whom it has been so long promised. It was projected three years ago, but its appearance has been delayed by causes that will be understood by every one who, in America, has undertaken to produce a costly, illustrated volume. Yet, this delay is not without a compensating advantage, for it has enabled the publishers to furnish an account of the Park in a state much nearer completion than it was when the book was first announced.

While this book has been designed, rather as a pleasure-book for the eye and the mind, than as a formal guide to the Park, it may safely be recommended for that purpose to those to whom its size is no objection, by the fulness of its details, and the accuracy of its facts.

One of our most popular artists, Mr. A. F. Bellows, has spent many months in making the drawings which add so much to the value of the work; our best engravers have employed their skill in cutting them on the wood; and the lovers of beautiful printing will easily recognize in the press-work the hand of Alvord.

AUTHOR'S PREFACE.

THE writer of the following pages cannot think his work complete without an expression of thanks to those gentlemen officially connected with the Central Park, to whom he is so much indebted for the means of securing whatever accuracy may be allowed to belong to his performance.

Although the Government of the Park is not in any way responsible for any statement contained in these pages other than such as are founded on its

Annual Reports, yet every facility has been cordially given to the writer to make himself acquainted with the topography of the Park, and with so much of its management as it was desirable or proper to communicate. And it certainly is not out of any desire to flatter the Commissioners that the belief is here expressed, that the more closely the management of this important undertaking is studied, the more it will appear that, disgraceful beyond all power of words adequately to express it as has been of late years the administration of the Government of the City of New York, yet the Commissioners of the Central Park have given our citizens all the proof that is needed that it is still possible to perform great public trusts with true economy, with unimpeachable honesty, and with a single, constant eye to the public good.

LIST OF ILLUSTRATIONS.

LIST OF ILLUSTRATIONS.

PLAN OF THE PARK.

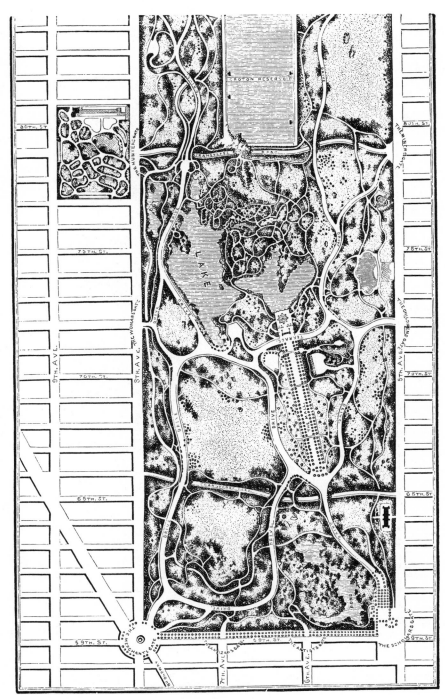

THE SOUTH END.

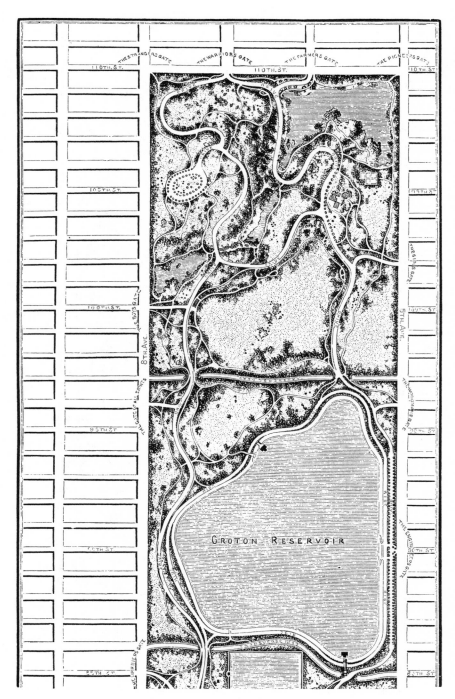

PLAN OF THE PARK.

THE NEW YORK CENTRAL PARK.

A GLANCE AT ITS HISTORY.

THIRTY or forty years ago, New York City must have had an almost rural aspect. This is especially true of what was then the upper part,—the region which lies between Canal Street and Prince Street;—but it will also apply to the extreme southern portion, the neighborhood of the Battery and Bowling-Green. For, even so late as 1840, the Battery was still a pleasant place, with grass and trees, and surrounded by a semicircle of handsome private houses, no longer lived in by fashionable people, perhaps, but rather by good, substantial folk who had resided in that neighborhood when it was in the highest fashion, and were loath to quit what was still a highly respectable quarter. No shops nor business houses had as yet intruded their unwelcome presence, but it was not long after the date we have mentioned, that the first symptoms of change began to appear in the transformation of one or two of the larger dwellings into boarding-houses of the better sort; and the neighborhood soon lost entirely its domestic character, and was abandoned to hotels, warehouses, and offices. Of course, in this change, the Battery and the Bowling-Green suffered equally with the houses. People gradually deserted them. The Battery, especially, which had once been the principal lounging place and promenade of fashionable New York, was abandoned for Broadway.

In the earlier period, before these changes began to take place, the inhabitants of the city did not want for places of recreation. The city proper covered but a small portion of the island, the line of the present Canal Street marking the northern boundary, and beyond this were large farms stretching up toward Harlem. To those who lived in the city itself, and who were not able to indulge in the luxury of a horse and chaise, the Battery and the Bowling-Green were sufficiently pleasant summer resorts, surrounded as they were by the residences of the gentry; but a walk in the fields was always easy to get; even Pearl Street and Maiden Lane were cheerful strolling-places; the boys skated on the canal, or swam in it, or made expeditions for nuts and apples to the large outlying farms.

Later, as the city grew, and the open country above the canal was invaded by houses and traversed by rudimentary streets, while, at the opposite end, the Battery and Bowling-Green began to yield a little to the demand of business men for room, there sprang up here and there public gardens, quiet places for refreshment and recreation; while open squares, such as the City Hall Park and St. John's Park, were laid out and planted with grass, and shrubbery, and trees—the one for public use, the other for a private playground and promenade. But even so late as 1825 the city was so sparsely built and town-gardens were so numerous—many of the houses being of wood, and standing detached, surrounded with shrubbery and trees—that parks or squares must have seemed unnecessary, for pleasant walks and strolls could be had in almost any quarter, and the upper part of the island abounded in delightful drives. There were also public gardens in plenty, both in the city itself and in the surrounding country, and the people were of that social, lively turn that they loved to frequent such places. Later, more formal gardens sprang up in the city, not, properly speaking, gardens at all, but mere open-air inclosures where people went to eat cakes and ices, the boys and girls to meet one another, and the elders to talk gossip and politics, and to discuss the scandal of the hour. Such gardens were "Vauxhall," in the Bowery, near Eighth Street; the "Bowery," so called from its beautiful over-arching trees, the prettiest part of the lower island; and "Contoits," a name that still thrills matronly bosoms, with a sigh for its remembered delights. "Niblo's" came later; we, ourselves, remember when it was really a garden, and occupied nearly the whole block of which it is now but an insignificant fragment. In the neighborhood of Twenty-first Street and

Broadway there lived at this time a good many English people, nearly all of them well-to-do merchants, having large gardens about their houses. These gentlemen were fond of flowers, and the tulip was a hobby with many of them. Every spring the splendor of these tulip-beds in full bloom would draw great numbers of people from the city to see them. In order to protect the flowers from the sun, they were shielded by large light awnings of cotton; and it must have been a pretty sight—the gay beds of brilliant, many-colored flowers, and the cheerful, chatting people walking about, discussing the merits of the several gardens under the bright spring sky.

The change that deprived New York of this rural character came not by slow and easily traced degrees, but suddenly. There are hundreds of people living who remember when the tide turned, and the city grew from a small town, almost in a night, like Jonah's gourd, to be the great metropolis it is to-day. The change came too suddenly for the city's good. It was not growth, it was revolution, and provision had to be made so speedily for the population that began to pour in about 1830, and which has continued to pour in steadily and with hardly any intermission from that day to this, that many things had to be done carelessly, many irretrievable blunders were committed, and opportunities lost that will never present themselves again. It was not long before people began to feel the change from the sparsely built city, with its open lots, its water-courses and gardens, to the narrowing streets, the long blocks of closely packed houses, and the small back-yards, where, at the best, a grape-vine and a pocket-handkerchief of grass could make out to grow. Old New Yorkers felt stifled, and young New York felt the need of play-ground, and of some substitute for the free life of the old days and of the active out-door employments it had so lately been able to enjoy.

After all, the city was not so badly off as might have been feared. There was Hoboken for a delightful walk or for active games, ball-playing, boating, bowling, and quoits. Staten Island, too, which, thirty years ago, was nearly covered with fine woods, and which is still one of the richest fields for the botanist that can be found within any reasonable distance of New York, was becoming a favorite resort for pic-nic parties and for boys on Saturday afternoons. Then there was the Bloomingdale Road, the delight of equestrians, for as yet it had not passed exclusively into the hands of rowdies and the horse-racing gentry ; while now that large and handsome steamboats were making the journey to Albany both swift and sure, the beauties of the Hudson River were gradually discovered, and the inhabitants of the already crowded city learned what a treasure of romantic scenery lay within easy reach.

The growth of the city was almost without precedent for suddenness, and the demand for building-ground became so great that it was with difficulty even the public squares, reserved for air and recreation, could be preserved inviolate. But building was the rage, and beside, it was the necessity of the time, and every new building meant so much less air, so much less light, so much less room for play, for rest, for ceremonial display. The Battery remained for some time longer a cheerful spot, green with grass and trees, and with a prospect such as could not easily be surpassed anywhere for variety and beauty. But no one now went to it for pleasure. Occasionally a military review would take place there, or the city officials would receive there some distinguished foreign visitor, but the more respectable citizens and the fashionable would either forego the ceremony and display altogether, or wait until the procession which usually terminated such affairs found its way into their cleaner and more elegant neighborhood.* The park, too, was gradually scrimped of its fair proportions, its lower end taken up by a fountain basin, out of all proportion to the space it occupies, and the upper part crowded with public offices, while the placards ordering people to keep off the grass became a standing joke, for, little by little, the grass had disappeared, the posts that supported the guarding-chains had rotted and been stolen, and the trees that had once adorned it seemed to

* Yet, what a truly noble entrance to New York City, the Battery might still be made ! In proper hands, Castle Garden might be transformed, and that at no extravagant expense, into a stately water-gate with an ample wharf of stone to which a steamer or a man-of-war could bring whatever honorable company might be the city's guest, and after due ceremonial reception within the inclosure, the procession of soldiery, officials, and citizens, would have free room to form on the broad esplanade of the Battery itself, no longer the squalid sleeping-place of beggars, and lounging-place of drones that it is now ; but bright with flowers, and over-arched with trees, well paved, well fenced ; as bright and sunny a spot, and with as noble an outlook as could be found in the world. New York owes it to herself to have such an entrance ; at present the only access to her is through unutterably filthy ways.

have no desire to outlive the decay of a spot which had once been the city's pride.

Retreat from the city for those who longed for a few hours' rest, for a breath of the open air, or for a sight of the sky, was cut off on nearly every side. Staten Island and Coney Island were too far away; Hoboken was no longer pleasant nor reputable; it had ceased to be a place of resort for those who sought a quiet stroll, with an ice or coffee under the trees of the Elysian Fields, and it had not yet attained to the dignity of a suburb. For several years the people of New York had seemed to be growing into a settled submission to this state of things—one, we may almost say, without precedent, for there is hardly another great city in the world that does not contain, either within its own boundaries or in its suburbs, the means of gratifying the desire of its inhabitants for an occasional escape from the confinement of city walls, and the hurry and bustle of the city streets. To tell the truth, New York, admirably placed as it is for commercial purposes, is far from being a convenient place to live in; to use an Irish bull, its centre is not in the middle, but at one end, and the time consumed in getting from home to business or pleasure is a great drawback to the enjoyment of the many material comforts which the city offers her citizens.

But the shape of a city, like the shape of a man's head, although it may stand greatly in the way of its improvement, and be much to be regretted, is a thing not to be altered, and the only matter to be considered is, how to make the best of it. And about the year 1848 the people of New York began to find that something must be done to supply the want, getting to be felt every day more and more, of space to walk abroad and recreate themselves. There was no place within the city limits in which it was pleasant to walk, or ride, or drive, or stroll; no place for skating, no water in which it was safe to row; no field for base-ball or cricket; no pleasant garden where one could sit and chat with a friend, or watch his children play, or, over a cup of tea or coffee, listen to the music of a good band. Theatres, concerts, and lectures were the only amusements within reach of the mass of the people; the side-walks, the balconies, the back-yards, the only substitutes for the Hyde Park or Tuileries of the Old World, or the ancient freedom and rural beauty of Young New York.

The public was discontented, but it had no means of giving expression to its feeling. The rich people, when they could not endure their *ennui* any longer, took ship, and went and walked in the Tuileries, or drove with the other nabobs in Hyde Park, or drank coffee under the lindens of Berlin, and came home when they felt like it. Or, if they did not share the common taste of American rich people for expatriation, they left the city and went " up the river," where they built ugly houses, costing fabulous sums, and tormented mother Earth with landscape gardening, tasteless enough to keep the houses in countenance, or threw their money away in gentlemanly farming. As for the people with small incomes, and the salaried class, they had to make up their minds, since the mountains would not come to them, to go once a year, for a week or two, to the mountains. It was then that the traditions of Saratoga and Newport were formed, and the city was nearly deserted in the summer by large numbers of the inhabitants. No person, who aspired to any rank in the fashionable world, was ever known to be in the city in July or August, and " not at home," if it did not mean " in Europe," meant " at a fashionable watering-place." Now, too, the suburban region about New York began to be invaded by a large class that found city-life expensive out of all proportion to its health, comfort, and opportunities for enjoyment, as well as by those, chiefly industrious mechanics, who found it impossible to lay up money while obliged to pay such rents as were coming to be demanded, or, indeed, to live with decency in the only houses that were to be obtained for rents that, in Europe, are asked for comfortable, nay, luxurious, rooms. The discomfort was widely felt, and it was to be expected that somebody would discover that he had a mission to put an end to it, or to spur other people to do so. And in 1848, Mr. A. J. Downing, in an article called " A Talk about Public Parks and Gardens," published in the *Horticulturist*, a journal which he edited at the time, gave the first expression to the want, which everybody at that time felt, of a great Public Park.

In a characteristic way, the Americans of the North had already attempted to provide places for public exercise, not to say amusement, by the establishment of great cemeteries in the vicinities of the larger cities. In 1831, Mt. Auburn, near Boston, was consecrated, and the example set in the laying-out and in the adornment of that beautiful place was soon followed by the people of Philadelphia at "Laurel Hill," and later by New York at "Greenwood." These cemeteries soon became famous over the whole country, and thousands of people visited them annually. They were among the chief attractions of the cities to which they belonged. No stranger visited either of these cities for pleasure or observation who was not taken to the cemeteries, nor was it long before the smaller cities, and even towns and villages began to set aside land and to lay it out for the double purpose of burying-ground and pleasure-ground. In 1848, when Mr. Downing wrote the "Talk about Public Parks and Gardens" which we have mentioned, these cemeteries were all the rage, and so deeply was the want felt which they supplied, and so truly beautiful were they in themselves, that it is not to be wondered at if people were slow to perceive that there was a certain incongruity between a graveyard and a place of recreation. The truth is, people were glad to get fresh air, and a sight of grass, and trees, and flowers, with, now and then, a pretty piece of sculpture, to say nothing of the drive to all this beauty, and back again, without considering too deeply whether it might not be better to have it all without the graves, and the funeral processions. Of course, at first, the sadder purpose of these places was not so conspicuous as it soon became. For several years after they were first laid out they were in reality parks and pleasure-grounds, with, here and there, a monument or tombstone half seen among the trees. But this could not last for long. The dead increase as the living do—

> "Every minute dies a man,
> Every minute one is born,"

and soon the small white tents grew thick along the paths and lanes, and the statelier houses of the rich and notable dead rose shining in the more conspicuous places, and the dark line of hearse and carriages was met at every turn, so that it was not easy even for the lightest hearted or the most indifferent to get much cheer out of a landscape set so thick with sad suggestions. And then the tide turned, and fashion and pleasure looked about for a garden where death was not so frequent a visitor.

In July, 1849, Mr. Downing published in the "Horticulturist" an essay on "Public Cemeteries and Public Gardens," which is mainly an enlargement of a paragraph in the "Talk about Public Parks and Gardens," and the object of which was to convince the public that a large public park in the vicinity of any one of the great Atlantic cities would not only be a great luxury, but a great material benefit to the inhabitants, and that it would pay its own expenses beside. "That such a project, carefully planned and liberally and judiciously carried out would not only *pay* in money, but largely civilize and refine the national character, foster the love of rural beauty, and increase the knowledge of, and taste for, rare and beautiful trees and plants, we cannot entertain a reasonable doubt. It is only necessary for one of the three cities which first opened cemeteries to set the example, and, the thing once fairly seen, it becomes universal. The true policy of republics is to foster the taste for great public libraries, parks, and gardens, which *all* may enjoy, since our institutions wisely forbid the growth of private fortunes sufficient to achieve these desirable results in any other way."

In 1850 Mr. Downing took a summer trip to England, leaving home in June and returning in October. He went, not merely for pleasure, but to see what had been done and what was then being done in the old world in architecture and landscape-gardening, that he might gather hints and suggestions for improvement in those arts among his countrymen at home. Naturally enough, he was more taken with the English exploits in landscape-gardening—with the Chatsworths and Woburn Abbeys—than with the modern architecture. But, greatly as he admired the splendid country-seats of the hereditary nobility of England, he perceived that the great wealth it required to support these enormous establishments raised these houses and grounds so far above ours that they are not directly or practically instructive to Americans. More interesting to him were the great public parks. In September, 1850, he wrote to the "Horticulturist" a letter from England on the London parks, in which, after a charmingly vivid description of those remarkable places, he concludes as follows : "We fancy, not without reason, in New York, that we have a great city, and that the introduction of Croton water is so marvellous a luxury in the way of health, that nothing more need be done for the comfort of half a million of people. In crossing the Atlantic, a young New Yorker who was rabidly patriotic, and who boasted daily of the superiority of our beloved commercial metropolis over every city on the globe, was our most amusing companion. I chanced to meet him one afternoon, a few days after we landed, in one of the great parks in London, in the midst of all the sylvan beauty and human enjoyment I have attempted to describe to you. He threw up his arms as he recognized me, and exclaimed: 'Good heavens! what a scene! and I took some Londoners to the steps of the City Hall last summer, to show them the Park of New York!' I consoled him with the advice to be less conceited thereafter in his cockneyism, and to show foreigners the Hudson and Niagara, instead of the City Hall and Bowling-Green. But the question may well be asked, ' Is New York really not rich enough, or is there absolutely not land enough in America, to give our citizens public parks of more than ten acres?' "

By this time, indeed, the question was getting quite generally asked. In all societies there was a demand for a place within the city limits, where people could walk, and drive, and ride, and skate, and row; where base-ball and cricket could be played, and all classes of the community find rest and recreation. We can imagine Downing's young cockney returning to New York, and telling his little circle at home of the astonishment and mortification he had felt on comparing the generous provision which the government of a monarchy had made for the enjoyment of its subjects, with the wretched way in which the free citizens of a great republic had stinted themselves. Every intelligent New Yorker that went abroad must have made the same comparison, and must have given expression to the same astonishment and mortification. And now that this widespread public feeling had found a voice in Mr. Downing, there needed nothing but that some person in authority, mayor, governor, or legislator, should recommend that the public need be provided for, to secure that something effectual should be done. And accordingly, in 1851, Mr. A. C. Kingsland, who was then Mayor of New York, sent a Message to the Common Council, in which the whole question was stated so clearly and succinctly, and the necessity for prompt and efficient action was so forcibly urged, that there is no wonder it took hold of the public attention, and became the leading topic of discussion in social circles and in the newspapers. As this Message is of importance in the history of the Central Park, and as it is buried in the not often explored storehouse of official documents of the city government, the reader will perhaps not think it out of place in a foot-note.*

The Message of Mayor Kingsland was sent to the Common Council on the fifth day of April, 1851, and was at once referred to the Com-

---

* *To the Honorable the Common Council:* —

GENTLEMEN—The rapid augmentation of our population, and the great increase in the value of property in the lower part of the city, justify me in calling the attention of your honorable body to the necessity of making some suitable provision for the wants of our citizens, who are thronging into the upper wards which, but a few years since, were considered as entirely out of the city. It seems obvious to me that the entire tongue of land south of the line drawn across the Park is destined to be devoted, entirely and solely, to commercial purposes; and the Park and Battery, which were formerly favorite places of resort for pleasure and recreation for citizens whose residences were below that line, are now deserted. The tide of population is rapidly flowing to the northern section of the island, and it is here that provision should be made for the thousands whose dwellings will, ere long, fill up the vacant streets and avenues north of Union Park.

The public places of New York are not in keeping with the character of our city; nor do they in any wise subserve the purpose for which such places should be set apart. Each year will witness a certain increase in the value of real estate, out of the city proper, and I do not know that any period will be more suitable than the present one for the purchase and laying out of a park on a scale which will be worthy of the city.

There are places on the island easily accessible, and possessing all the advantages of wood, lawn, and water, which might, at a comparatively small expense, be converted into a park which would be at once the pride and ornament of the city. Such a park, well laid out, would become the favorite resort of all classes. There are thousands who pass the day of rest among the idle and dissolute, in porter-houses or in places more objectionable, who would rejoice in being enabled to breathe the pure air in such a place, while the ride and drive through its avenues, free from the noise, dust, and confusion inseparable from all thoroughfares, would hold out strong inducements for the affluent to make it a place of resort.

There is no park on the island deserving the name, and while I cannot believe that any one can be found to advance an objection against the expediency of having such a one in our midst, I think that the expenditure of a sum necessary to procure and lay out a park of sufficient magnitude to answer the purposes above mentioned would be well and wisely appropriated, and would be returned to us fourfold in the health, happiness, and comfort of those whose interests are specially intrusted to our keeping—the poorer classes.

The establishment of such a park would prove a lasting monument to the wisdom, sagacity, and forethought of its founders, and would secure the gratitude of thousands yet unborn for the blessings of pure air, and the opportunity for innocent, healthful enjoyment.

I commend this subject to your consideration, in the conviction that its importance will insure your careful attention and prompt action.

A. C. KINGSLAND, Mayor.

mittee on Lands and Places. This committee soon after returned a report favorable to the Mayor's views, and recommending that application should be made to the Legislature to appropriate that portion of New York Island known as Jones's Wood to the uses of a public park, this seeming to the committee better adapted for the purpose than any other situation.

Jones's Wood is a tract of undulating ground lying along the shore of the East River, and was at that time for the most part unoccupied by buildings, though here and there were still standing a few of those old-fashioned "mansions," as they were somewhat grandiloquently called, which, in former times, had been the country-seats of wealthy New York merchants retired from business, but most of which have of late years been abandoned and are fast going to decay. The land which it was proposed to take for a park extended from the East River to the Third Avenue, and from Sixty-sixth Street, on the south, to Seventy-fifth Street, on the north, and contained about one hundred and fifty acres. The advantages it offered for the purposes of a park were, the irregularity of its surface, its nearness to the East River, always an animated scene, with its steamboats, shipping, the islands, and the neighboring shore; and there was, beside, what, by most people, was thought would prove a great gain in time and expense, a thick growth of trees over nearly the whole region.

The Legislature, at an extra session, held in 1851, following the recommendation of the Common Council, passed an Act, known as the Jones's Wood Park Bill, dated the 11th of July, authorizing the city, after certain prescribed estimates, examinations, and formalities had been gone through with, to take possession of the tract in question. But hardly had this Act been published than there arose such a strenuous opposition to the proposed site, that the Board of Aldermen appointed (August 5th, 1851) a special committee to look into the matter and report upon the advantages and disadvantages of the ground designated in the Act of the Legislature, and also to examine whether there were not some locality within the city limits better suited to the purpose of a public park. This committee, consisting of Messrs. Daniel Dodge and Joseph Britton, made a very full report, strongly recommending a tract in the centre of the island for the site of the Park in preference to Jones's Wood, on considerations of its greater extent and convenience of access, its general availability, and its proportionally far less cost. Among the influences that worked to secure the present site to the city, this able report was doubtless one of the strongest. It put the whole case clearly before the public, stating the argument at length, yet without waste words, and gave voice to a wide-spread popular preference for a more central locality, which had thus far found no expression except through the newspapers. Its recommendations were adopted by the Board of Aldermen, and on the report being referred to the Legislature, that body passed an Act on the 21st of July, 1853,* authorizing the city to take possession of the ground now known as the Central Park.

The Act of 1851, called the Jones's Wood Park Bill, had never gone into effect, because the Supreme Court, on account of alleged material errors in the Bill, had refused to appoint commissioners ; but the owners of that property, not willing to lose the opportunity of selling their land to so good a customer as the city, again bestirred themselves in the matter, and to such good purpose, that they actually persuaded the Legislature to stultify itself by passing, on the same day, July 21st, 1853, two separate Acts, one, mentioned above, authorizing the taking of land in the centre of the island for the Central Park, the other giving authority to the city to take possession of Jones's Wood. But the opinion of the public was too plainly in favor of the central site, and the next year, April 11th, 1854, the Act relative to Jones's Wood was repealed, and no further attempt was made to revive it.

On the 17th of November, 1853, the Supreme Court, by Judge William Mitchell, appointed five commissioners of estimate and assessment to take the land for the Central Park. These commissioners were William Kent, Michael Ulshoeffer, Luther Bradish, Warren Brady, and Jeremiah Towle, all gentlemen well known to the community, and in whom a wide confidence was felt that their difficult task would be performed with fairness and judgment. Nor did this confidence prove to have been ill-grounded. The commissioners employed nearly three years in the work of estimating and assessing, sending in their report on the 4th of October, 1856, and, as Judge

---

* Misprinted "July" 23d" in First Annual Report, Jan. 1, 1867, pp. 6 and 7.

Harris remarked in confirming their report, it is an evidence of the success with which their difficult task had been performed, that but about one in forty of the owners of the lots taken for the Park appeared before him to object to the award of the commissioners. Mr. Fernando Wood, who, as the city has reason to remember, was at that time Mayor, took occasion, in a message to the Common Council, referring to another matter, to allude to the length of time the commissioners were consuming in their business. "The whole scope of their duties appears to me," says this model citizen and magistrate, "to be very simple, and easily accomplished. I do not see why they should consume so much time." But when it is considered that the commissioners had to hear and decide upon the claims of the owners of seven thousand five hundred lots; and that in many of these cases there were involved the interests of minors and orphans, and of persons who might be seriously crippled in their resources by an adverse decision (and Judge Harris, in confirming their report, admits that, although the action of the commissioners was pre-eminently judicious and equitable, yet there were cases of individual hardship); when we consider, too, that, as to most of the lots, it was rather their prospective than their present value that had to be estimated, a consideration that greatly increased the difficulty of passing judgment, and made the award liable to much bitterness of suspicion; and, beside this, if we remember that it was not only the giving of money that they had to attend to, but the taking it away, for they had not only to appraise the value of the lots absorbed into the Park, but to tax those that lay about it as well, in view of the advantage they were to gain by their nearness to it; when all these things are looked at, the time consumed in untangling all these snarled and knotted skeins appears by no means unreasonably long. At all events, the Supreme Court confirmed this report of the commissioners without hesitation, after a careful examination had convinced it that substantial justice had been done, and on the 5th of February, 1856, the Comptroller announced to the Common Council that, as by the Act of 1853 the payment of the awards to the owners of the lots, and of the expenses of the commissioners must be made immediately on the confirmation of their report, it had become their duty to make an appropriation to meet those charges. Accordingly, an ordinance was passed for the payment of five million, one hundred and sixty-nine thousand, three hundred and sixty-nine dollars and ninety cents, of which sum one million, six hundred and fifty-seven thousand, five hundred and ninety dollars were to be paid by the owners of lands adjacent to the Park, in view of the benefit they would receive from their neighborhood to it.

Thus the Central Park became the possession of the city, the greatest blessing that had been bestowed upon it since the building of the great aqueduct. Not quite five years had elapsed since it was first proposed by Mayor Kingsland, and it seems to us that, when the difficulty of adjusting so many private claims and conflicting interests as are involved in the purchase of over seven thousand lots on the very border of a large and rapidly growing town is considered, it cannot be denied that, in the steady persistence with which it was pursued, the enterprise was an exception to the common fate of such undertakings. There was an unusual unanimity in the public mind from the first as to the need of a large public park, and even the dispute as to location did not delay matters long. No doubt, it would have been much more difficult to secure so large a tract of land if it had been thickly strewn with buildings; the reason why the Jones's Wood party pushed their cause so persistently was, that the private interests at stake were so much greater than in the case of the unoccupied lots of the Central Park, and the owners of houses and lots along the East River were much more eager to have the public purchase their property than were those who owned uncleared and unimproved land in the middle of the island. The public, however, was quite as shrewd as they, and, in spite of all their blandishments, chose the better situation. This danger was easily escaped, but, at the very last, while the commissioners appointed by the Supreme Court were yet engaged in their labors, a vigorous effort was made by persons owning land on the southern boundary of the Central Park to have its dimensions curtailed at that end; and so well did they play their cards, that the Common Council was actually induced to pass a resolution, April 3d, 1854,* asking the Legislature to change the southern

---

* In the First Annual Report on the Improvement of the Central Park, appendix M., p. 130, this date is wrongly printed 1853. The Act which it was proposed to amend was not passed till July 21, 1853.

line of the Park, making it at Seventy-second, instead of at Fifty-ninth Street, and only the emphatic veto of Mayor Wood saved the public from the annoyance and expense of this further delay. Mr. Wood's public record is every way so unhandsome, that we are glad to be able to give him credit for at least one creditable act. This threatened trouble having once blown over, there seems to have been no further opposition, and, as we have seen, the purchase of the Park was at length completed.

Mr. Egbert L. Viele, the engineer by whom the land for the Central Park was first surveyed, intimates, in his report to the commissioners (1857), that secret influences worked with the Legislature to hinder further action in getting the park improvement under way ; and very possibly this may have been so, although it is difficult to see what malcontents could have hoped to do in opposition to the decisive steps already taken by the constituted authorities, acting in obedience to the clearly expressed will of the major part of the people. But, for some reason or other, hard at this late day to discover, the Legislature did nothing looking toward a government for the Park, and hence, on the 19th of May, 1856, the Board of Aldermen adopted an ordinance appointing the Mayor and the Street Commissioner commissioners with full authority to govern the Park, to determine upon a plan for its improvement, and to appoint such persons as they might see fit to carry out their intentions. Mr. Fernando Wood and Mr. Joseph S. Taylor, the then Street Commissioner, thus empowered, entered at once and with commendable spirit upon the discharge of their duties. Feeling that their position was one of great responsibility and difficulty, they determined to seek the best advice they could obtain from men whose public and social position, with their reputation for taste and judgment, would give their opinions weight. They therefore invited Washington Irving, George Bancroft, James E. Cooley, Charles F. Briggs, James Phalon, Charles A. Dana, and Stewart Brown to attend the meetings of the commission and form a board of consultation for the purpose of discussing what course had best be pursued in order to secure a suitable design for laying out the Park. The first of these meetings was held on the

29th of May, 1856. Mr. Irving was made president of the Board, and the preliminaries were settled for carrying out the objects of the commission. At subsequent meetings various plans for the improvement of the Park were presented to them, but, on the whole, little was accomplished until the design sent in by Mr. Egbert L. Viele, the engineer of the Park, and strongly backed by Mayor Wood, was adopted. This seemed to be an important point gained, but, fortunately for the city, it resulted in nothing. No money was appropriated for the use of the commissioners, and we were thus saved the mortification of seeing all the labor that had been expended in securing the Park thrown away, and all the hopes that had been held of its beauty disappointed by the adoption of a commonplace and tasteless design.

The first annual report of the engineer of the Central Park was sent to the commissioners, January 1st, 1857. It forms Document No. 5 of the Proceedings of the Board of Aldermen for that year, and beside a history of the Park up to the time when the report was sent in, it contained a lithograph of Mr. Viele's plan and a full description of it. This plan would hardly be worth speaking of to-day, if there had not been at one time a persistent effort made to convince the public that the plan afterward adopted—the one designed by Olmsted and Vaux, was a plagiarism, in, at least, two essential points, from that of Mr. Viele. It is very much to be regretted that such a charge as this should ever have been permitted to be made; for while any one, who felt sufficient interest in the matter, to investigate it, could easily have satisfied himself that the accusation had no foundation in fact, it was by no means easy for the public to know on which side the right lay. As the first report of the engineer to the then Commissioners of the Park (Messrs. Wood and Taylor) has long been out of print, we cannot refer the reader to it for an explanation of the difference between Mr. Viele's plan and the one afterward adopted. We may, however, state, in a few words, what were the main features of the design after which it was at first proposed to lay out the Park, describing them from the official copy of Mr. Viele's own drawing contained in his report, which is now before us. To be frank, this plan, about which so much was at one time written, is just such a matter-of-fact, tasteless affair as is always produced by engineers (begging pardon of the whole useful body), when they attempt any thing in the way of ornamental design. No thought was required to make it, and no other knowledge than a mere acquaintance with the topography of the ground to be worked. There is not a single difficulty overcome, a single advantage improved, a single valuable or striking improvement suggested. The roads follow the natural levels as far as possible, the existing water-courses are allowed to remain as they are, except that in two or three places the waters of marshy spots are collected into pools, and this, literally, is the only appearance of any intention to do any thing for the sake of beauty or picturesqueness. As for the arrangement of the roads, nothing could be more simple, and, at the same time, nothing could be more uninteresting. A drive, ninety feet wide, starts from the corner of Fifty-ninth Street and the Fifth Avenue, skirts the boundary of the Park, keeping as close to it as possible, cuts round the new Reservoir to the opposite side, and running along nearly parallel with the Eighth Avenue, leaves the Park at the southwest corner. This drive, Mr. Viele calls, "The Circuit," and it is one of the two "ideas" which his newspaper advocates charged the present plan with having borrowed from him: we shall see later with how little reason. After having followed the "Circuit," unless the visitor then took "The Glen Road," leading in a nearly direct line from a point between the Sixth and Seventh Avenues to the smaller Reservoir, he would see nothing more of the Park than he might have seen if he had gone up the Fifth Avenue, and down the Eighth. The other "idea" which the present plan was charged with having borrowed from Mr. Viele, is that of the transverse roads for traffic. Now, these transverse roads are indispensable, considering the situation of the Park, and the shape of the city. Take them away; prevent carts, wagons, omnibuses, from crossing the Park anywhere between the streets that bound it on the north and south, and you make two separate cities, one on either side. To put transverse roads into the plan, if, indeed, they had not been expressly called for by the instructions of the Commissioners to the competitors, was a natural notion enough; it might have occurred to anybody. But anybody, one would have thought, could also have seen that unless some way were devised, at the same time, of having, and not having them: of getting the good, and avoiding the evil of them, the Park would be seriously injured.

No other way occurred to Mr. Viele, nor, indeed, to any of the competitors but the successful ones, but just to lay transverse roads across his plan on a level with the surface like all the other roads in the Park. It must be plain at a glance that this arrangement would have destroyed the pleasure of driving or walking in the Park, to say nothing of its want of elegance. As we shall see, the authors of the successful plan, by a method as simple as it was ingenious, secured every thing that was needed for the accommodation of traffic, while, at the same time, they secured the privacy and comfort of visitors. Their plan in no way impaired the beauty of the Park nor interfered with its utility.

It was soon found that unless either the Legislature or the city authorities took more active measures for the government and improvement of the Park, the enterprise must fail of being carried out in a creditable manner; and, accordingly, on the 17th of April, 1857, the Legislature appointed a new Commission, consisting of eleven members, who were to hold office for five years, and who were empowered to expend a sum of money the interest of which should not exceed thirty thousand dollars. To raise this money the Common Council of the city issued stock having thirty years to run, which was immediately taken up by the public.

One of the first acts of the new Commission was, to lay aside the plan of Mr. Viele, and to advertise for new plans, to be sent in, in competition. The time at first fixed upon up to which plans could be sent in was the 1st of March, but it was afterwards extended, at the request of numerous persons intending to compete, to the 1st of April, at which time thirty-three plans had been sent in. These plans were placed in a room on Broadway that had been hired for the purpose, and from that time until the 21st of April the Board frequently held its meetings there, in order to facilitate a careful examination and thorough discussion of the merits of the several plans. On the 21st of April the Commissioners met to decide upon the choice of a plan, and on the first voting, No. 33, bearing the motto "Greensward," was declared, by the ballots of seven members out of the eleven, to be entitled to the first prize of two thousand dollars. The other prizes were awarded with more difficulty. The roll had to be called four times before it could be decided which was the second-best design, entitled to a prize of one thousand dollars, and an almost equal difficulty was met with in fixing upon the competitors deserving of the third and fourth prizes. Indeed, the excellence of "Greensward" had been easily seen to be pre-eminent, from the first, and yet, at one time, it ran a chance of being thrown out of the competition, for, on the very day of decision, two of the members of the Board endeavored to get rid of it by ingenious stratagems. One protested against its being even considered, on the ground that in his opinion the plan was not received by the Board on the 1st day of April, but on the 2d, and too late to entitle it to a premium according to the terms of the advertisement. This protest was laid on the table, only the mover and one other Commissioner voting in favor of it. Then that other Commissioner moved that there was no plan entitled to the first prize, but this, too, was lost. It was plain that the majority had settled with unanimity on this plan, and were determined to give it the preference. And, indeed, it well deserved it, as the public freely admitted when it was exhibited to them, and as time has since abundantly proved.

The authors of "Greensward," the successful plan, proved to be Mr. Frederick Law Olmsted and Mr. Calvert Vaux: both well known and highly esteemed by a large and cultivated circle in this community.

Mr. Olmsted, young as he was, had already a national reputation. He is an American of Americans, was long a successful practical farmer, and while still engaged in that pursuit had published a remarkable little book, the record of a vacation ramble, called "Walks and Talks of an American Farmer in England." But he had, since that time, become more widely known by his letters to the "New York Times" newspaper, written during a tour through the Southern States, under the signature of "Yeoman," and afterwards published in a volume— "The Sea-board Slave States." This book contained the first reliable account of the condition of society in the South, especially in the regions away from the great cities, that had, up to that time, been published in the North. It was written in so manly, straightforward a style, with such an evident determination to the plain, unvarnished truth, that it carried conviction with it, and no less won a wide public respect for the character of the writer. We speak of it here, because the qualities that made it were qualities that showed themselves later, when Mr. Olmsted filled the position of Superintendent of the Park, and Architect-in-Chief. The public will never know all that it owes in the possession of the Park to Mr. Olmsted's vigor; to his quiet, earnest zeal; to his integrity, and to the abundance of his resources. Few Americans in our time have shown so great administrative abilities.

Mr. Calvert Vaux is an Englishman by birth and training, who came to this country, and adopted it for his permanent home, in 1852. He left England on the invitation of Mr. Downing, to whom he had been highly recommended as the person best fitted to assist him in his profession of architect and landscape-gardener. He established himself at Newburg, as Mr. Downing's partner in business, and on the untimely death of that gentleman in 1853, he succeeded to his large and profitable clientage. At the time of the acceptance of his and Mr. Olmsted's design for the Park, he was already known as a skilful architect, and as the author of a valuable work on the subject of Domestic Architecture. It would hardly have been possible to find in our community two men better fitted by education, by experience, and by a combination of valuable qualities, to carry out so difficult and so important an undertaking as that of the Central Park. Perhaps it was not a mere piece of good luck that brought them together, and that swayed the Commissioners so unanimously in favor of their work, but a sort of fate which easily brings like to mate with like, and makes the fruit of such a union its own best praise.

THE CENTRAL PARK.

THE authors of "Greensward," when they sent in their plan, accompanied it with a small printed pamphlet explanatory of its main features, and of the general principles that had guided them in the design. This pamphlet has recently, after an interval of ten years, been reprinted, and one cannot but be struck in reading it with the evidence it gives of a thorough understanding on the part of its authors, both of what the public needed in a Park of this character, and how its needs could most perfectly be met. This reprint contains two wood-cuts: one, of the original design, and the other of the Park in its present condition, showing how far the original design has been carried out, and how far it has been modified and improved upon. On examining these two plans, we shall find that, except at the north, where the extension of the boundary line from 106th to 110th Street rendered an entire revision of the original design in the upper portion necessary, the plan, in its main features, is the same in 1868 that it was in 1858. Such differences as will be observed are, nearly all, what may be called external, relating to the widening of the streets that surround the Park, the grading of the avenues, and the improvement of the several approaches. In almost every case, too, the changes and improvements that have been made were strongly recommended in this report, and have been found necessary by experience. This is especially worthy of remark because it gives us a warrant that this important work is being carried out with deliberation and thoughtful care. It was originally planned with an intelligence and foresight that made nothing necessary but to develop the design, and ten years' use of the Park by the public has sufficiently proved its excellence.* A glance at the Plan, before beginning our running description of the Park in detail, will enable us to understand it better. It will be seen that the whole area is naturally divided into two clearly defined but unequal parts by the prominent transverse ridge lying between 74th Street and 97th Street, which is still further emphasized by the old and new Reservoirs, two immense structures, whose existence ought, in our opinion, to have been a powerful argument against the selection of this particular tract for the site of the Central Park. Large as the Park appears to us to-day, it will at no very distant time appear too small for the number of people who will make use of it, and the withdrawal of 136 acres, the united area of the two Reservoirs, from the 768 acres, which is the whole number contained within the bounding lines of the Park is a serious drawback. It is, however, of no use to find fault at this late day with the choice of site, and the Commissioners have done wisely in endeavoring to make the most of what has been put into their hands; and, so well have Messrs. Olmsted and Vaux managed with the ground on either side of these Reservoirs, that we may say the smaller one—the old Reservoir—is hardly felt any longer as an obstacle. The Park is divided into two distinct parts, then, by the new Reservoir alone. Let us, first, consider the lower of these two divisions. It has been taken for granted—it certainly might reasonably have been taken for granted in 1858—that the great throng of visitors must, for a long time, enter the Park from the region below 59th Street. And, accordingly, the two principal entrances of the southern half of the Park have been made, the one, at the southeastern angle—Fifth Avenue and Fifty-ninth Street—

		Pedestrians.	Equestrians.	Vehicles.
* In 1862, there visited the Park,	......	1,996,918	71,645	709,010
" 1864, " " "	....	2,295,199	100,397	1,148,161
" 1866, " " "	....	3,412,892	86,757	1,519,808
" 1867, " " "	....	2,998,770	84,994	1,381,697

and the other at the southwestern angle—Eighth Avenue and Fif-ty-ninth Street. We will enter the Park at the former of these gateways, and leave it by the other, but it will be observed that the road starting from either of these entrances leads naturally toward the interior of the Park, and in every legitimate way avoids playing the part of a mere skirting or circuit road. The principal defect of the Park site is its disproportioned length, and it is especially de-sirable that the visitor's attention should be called as little as possible to the boundaries east and west, which, when the best has been done, are found very difficult to keep out of sight. Every one of the competing designs except " Greensward " made the circuit-drive, keeping as close to the boundaries as possible, a prominent feature, and, probably, for the reasons that it was thought best by the de-signers, not only to secure as long a drive as the size of the Park would admit, but to have as large a space as possible in the middle of the tract free, or comparatively free, for those who came to the Park not to drive, but to walk, or stroll, or play. Messrs. Olmsted and Vaux alone saw that the boundary line must be avoided ; but, they also saw that the enjoyment of one class of visitors must not be allowed to interfere with that of any other. The first of these principles made them lead their drive at once toward the centre, and even on the west side, where it assumes more the character of a circuit-drive, it will be observed that the curves continually lead in, and that the road, in its whole length, approaches very near the boundary but once or twice, and then only when obliged to do so by the new Reservoir and by the western end of the lake. The second of these principles has been acted upon in the ingenious ar-rangement by which the drives, bridle-paths, and walks are kept entirely separate and distinct, so that visitors desiring to enjoy either recreation, may do so without interference. The whole Park may be enjoyed by any one, whether in his carriage, on horseback, or on foot ; and, though ingenuity always reaches its end at the least ex-pense, yet no necessary expense has been spared to carry out this admirable part of the Park system as perfectly as is possible. The drives in the Park vary in width, the widest being sixty feet, and the narrowest forty-five; they are followed in their whole length by walks for pedestrians, but there are a great number of these walks that avoid the carriage-road altogether. The bridle-path is twenty-five feet wide, and, in the southern half of the Park, runs a course quite independent of the drive, but in the northern half, the equestrian has the choice, at present, of turning into the drive after passing the old Reservoir and leaving it again after making the circuit of that portion, or of shortening his run by rounding the Reservoir, and so home. Meanwhile children, pedestrians, and old or young who come with a book, with knitting, or merely to sit and look on the scene, have, free from interruption either by carriage or horsemen, the Mall, the Terrace, the Ramble, the many picturesque and comfortable summer-houses, and the border walk about the inland sea of the new Reservoir.

THE LAKE NEAR FIFTH AVENUE AND FIFTY-NINTH STREET.

Immediately on entering the southeastern gateway—Fifth Avenue and Fifty-ninth Street—we see on our left hand an irregular piece of water with banks of considerable steepness. This is called "The Pond." It is about five acres in extent, and, like all the wa-

ter-pieces in the Park, is largely artificial, advantage being taken of
the natural drainage of the ground.　On the western side the banks
project boldly into the water, thus giving it a sort of crescent shape,
and, by dividing it into two parts, adding greatly to its variety.　The
banks are quite picturesque ; here, a bold bluff on the eastern side
answers to the rocks on the west; here a broad grassy slope de-
scends to the very edge of the water, and on the southern side a
sandy beach enables the children to watch the ducks and swans.
In the skating season this Pond makes a capital chapel-of-ease to
the larger Terrace Lake, and hundreds of skaters stop here at the
entrance to the Park in preference to taking the additional walk,
and joining the larger crowd.　As we pass the Pond we see the

THE ARSENAL.

Arsenal on our right, a large, and by no means handsome building,
formerly owned by the State, but purchased by the City in 1856
for the sum of $275,000.　This purchase included, of course, the
ground on which the Arsenal stands, and it was shortly afterward
taken possession of by the Commissioners, and used for various
purposes.　The lower stories served for lumber rooms, and in the
upper part the large staff of architects and engineers' draughtsmen
found rough-looking, but, on the whole, very pleasant quarters.

Perhaps, however, we shall not be far wrong if we fancy the Arsenal to have proved as troublesome a gift to the Commissioners as the elephant was to the bewildered man who drew him in a lottery. The Arsenal is a very large building, and is very poorly built. It is a parallelogram with an octagonal tower at each angle, and two side entrances, each flanked by towers. None of these are in reality towers at all, but mere octagonal projections from the walls; they are nevertheless carried above the roof, which is flat, and, in order to complete the resemblance to towers, they are finished on the inner side with wood. All the building, as all the work of every kind, that has been done in the Park, is of so solid and excellent a sort, that it must be a perpetual annoyance to the Commissioners to have such a flimsy, make-believe structure as this on their hands. There have been various propositions to make it serve some useful purpose. At one time there was talk of the Historical Society taking it, and transferring thither their collections. This intention has, we believe, been abandoned, partly because the Historical Society is not yet in a pecuniary condition to avail itself of the opportunity, but principally, we suspect, because the Commission has determined that the establishment of institutions, whether literary or scientific, within the Park, ought not to be encouraged, on account of its limited area. The proper place for our Historical Societies, Museums of Natural History, Collections of Antiquities, Libraries, and Picture Galleries, will be on the avenues that border the Park, or better still, on squares opening out of those avenues. Of late, the Arsenal building has been used as a place of deposit for the somewhat incongruous "gifts" that are made to the Park every year. Here are deposited several of the designs of the original competition; among them the curious model made by Mrs. Parrish, to illustrate the design she sent in on paper. In the second story are a number of stuffed animals, and on the ground-floor a small but interesting collection of living ones. There are also cages containing eagles, foxes, prairie-dogs, and bears, outside the building, but it is hoped that before long sufficient progress will have been made with the grounds of the Zoological Garden—on the western side of the Eighth Avenue, between 77th and 81st streets—to allow of all the animals belonging to the Park being removed to quarters expressly designed for them, and suited to their comfort and well-being.

Just before reaching the Arsenal the bridle-road and foot-path, which, for a short distance have run parallel, diverge : the one turning sharp to the west and running under the carriage-road, which spans it by a handsome bridge of Albert sandstone, the other keep-

BRIDGE OVER THE BRIDLE PATH NEAR ARSENAL.

ing due north, passing the Arsenal, and a little beyond it going under one of the transverse traffic-roads, to which we have before alluded. There are four of these transverse roads in the whole length of the Park : one at Sixty-fifth Street ; another at Seventy-ninth ; a third at Eighty-fifth Street, on the Fifth Avenue, but as it follows the curved southern wall of the new Reservoir, this road comes out at Eighty-sixth Street on the Eighth Avenue. The fourth road is at Ninety-seventh Street. The original instructions to the competitors called for these transverse roads, but no one of the designs, excepting "Greensward," offered any solution to the very serious problem presented by the necessity of making provision for the traffic that

must at some day be provided with roadway across the Park, and
which must yet, at the same time, be prevented from interfering
with the objects for which the Park has been created. All the
other competitors merely carried their transverse roads from one
side of the Park to the other, on the surface, keeping the same level
with the other roads, and not in any way to be distinguished from
them. Of course, such an arrangement as this would have even
now been sufficient to interfere seriously with the comfort, the re-
tirement, and even the safety of the Park. What would it have
been in twenty years, when the steadily advancing flood of houses
and shops, with their swarms of inhabitants, shall have broken
against the southern boundary of the Park, crowded up the narrow
territory on either side, and met again, to spread over the whole
northern end of the island? Messrs. Olmsted and Vaux early saw

THE MALL, LOOKING UP.

this difficulty, and devised the plan, which was at once adopted, of
carrying these transverse roads below the level of the Park surface.

The only place where any one of these traffic-roads goes over, instead of under, the other roads of the Park, is at the point we have just mentioned, near the Arsenal, where the foot-path passes under an archway of Albert sandstone, with abutments of stone and a railing of iron supported by stone posts. Meanwhile, the carriage-road, crossing the bridle-path by the stone bridge shown in the cut, crosses this same traffic-road by a bridge whose architecture is nearly concealed by the shrubbery—for, whenever it has been possible to do so, the architects have endeavored to keep the existence of the traffic-roads out of mind, as well as out of sight—and in a few minutes reaches the southern end of the Mall.

The Mall is a straight walk leading, from a point just beyond the first traffic-road, where the roads starting from the Eighth and the Fifth Avenues meet, to the architectural structure called "The Terrace." It is one thousand two hundred and twelve feet in length and thirty-five feet in width, and is planted in its whole extent with a double row of American elms. It is intended to serve both for a promenade and a resting-place; the ground has been carefully constructed to be pleasant to the foot, and comfortable seats are placed at frequent points. At a point near the southern end of the Mall, between the last two elms on the eastern side, is the site where the proposed statue of Shakespeare is to be erected. The stone on which the pedestal is to be placed was laid with appropriate ceremonies on Saturday, the 23d of April, 1864, that day being the three hundreth anniversary of the poet's birth. The proposition to erect this memorial was made by Messrs. James H. Hackett, Esq., William Wheatley, Esq., Edwin Booth, Esq., and Hon. Charles P. Daly, on behalf of the Shakespeare Dramatic Association. The public have been appealed to for contributions, and have liberally responded, so that the statue, which has been designed by one of our best sculptors, J. Q. A. Ward, Esq., will, before long, be added to the attractions of the Park. Although we are not able to present our readers with an engraving of this statue, since it has not yet left the artist's studio, we may venture to assert that, not merely as a work of art, but as a psychological study of the man, Shakespeare, founded as it is on a careful analytical study of the Stratford bust and of the Droeshout engraving, it can hardly fail to be of value, and may give us, what it would be very pleasant to have, a standard imaginary statue of Shakespeare.

One of the two drives starting from the Eighth Avenue entrance joins the drive we have been thus far following from the Fifth Avenue, but, as will be seen by a reference to the Plan, they again diverge, the one keeping to the left of the Mall, and the other to the right of it. Our road continues, winding a little, but without any sharp turns, until it reaches the new Reservoir; but there are

THE FOOT-PATH BY WILLOWS, SOUTH-EAST OF THE MALL.

several points which we pass before getting so far, and as we are not confined to a literal vehicle in this imaginary visit of ours we can stop and look about us at our leisure.

At a short distance from the southern end of the Mall the drive crosses the bridge shown in our cut, a neat structure of dark red brick, the masonry of which, like all the masonry in the Park, is the very best of its kind. Looking over the bridge at the left, we see a group of large old willows, evidently ancient denizens of this region. When the Commissioners first took the Park lands in hand they found very few trees of any considerable size growing on this nearly barren tract, but they very jealously preserved all that they did find. Among them were these willows, and there were, here and there, other specimens of the same tree, which we shall meet with further on. There are also a few oaks of good size near the Casino, and a small group of pines on the lawn west of the Mall. It may be remembered that one of the principal recommendations of the Jones's Wood site for the Park was the large and flourishing growth of forest trees that nearly covered that tract of land, whereas the site of the Central Park was rocky and marshy, and not only had few trees, but had scarcely any thing that deserved the name of shrubbery. But, after consulting with all the gardeners who had had experience in the matter, the weight of evidence seemed to be against the practice of cutting walks and drives through old woodland where it is found necessary to fell much of the standing timber. And although it was plain that it would be necessary to wait a considerable time before any very striking or satisfactory result could be looked for from young plantations, it was decided to take the barren tract—the sheet of white paper, and write the future Park poem upon that. The popular desire, very loudly and impatiently expressed, for large trees, drove the Commissioners into planting the Mall with elms too far advanced in growth to be moved with safety. This was done by contract with a person who agreed to demand pay for only such trees as lived, and the result of the first year's planting was that a large number of the trees not only on the Mall but in other parts of the Park died, though the most considerable planting had been along the Mall. Since that time the experiment of moving large trees has been abandoned, and the public has ceased worrying the Commissioners into trying to circumvent nature.

The bridge by the willows, which we have just passed over, is very prettily constructed within, having seats in niches at the sides, which give grateful cooling rest on a sultry day, and in one of these niches is a fountain basin, where a draught of cold water can at all times be procured.

As we near Seventy-second Street our carriage-road divides, or, rather, sends off two branches. One of these is a mere outlet to Seventy-second Street; the other leads to the "Terrace," the central object of interest in the lower park. It will be discovered, however, by looking at the Plan, that the roads at this point are so arranged as to secure an almost direct communication across the Park

from the Fifth to the Eighth Avenue. A similar arrangement exists at One Hundred and Second Street, but it is not made as easy to cross here as at the lower transverse, because the neighborhood of the Park at that point does not make it desirable to establish this sort of communication as yet. But it is evident that, as the city grows, it will become necessary to increase the facilities for crossing the Park, either on foot, or in vehicles, whether for pleasure or from necessity. For mere business communi-

DRINKING FOUNTAIN.

cation between the two sides of the city, divided as it will be for a distance of more than two miles and a half by the Park—

the four traffic-roads afford all the facilities that will probably be needed. These are for carts and wagons of all descriptions, for fire-engines, for funerals—no funeral procession is allowed to enter the Park proper—and for all vehicles that are not suited to a place of the character which ought to be maintained in a large public pleasure-ground. Yet, it will easily be seen that, for many purposes, it may be highly desirable to have easy access from one side of the city to the other without being obliged to use the traffic-roads, for, these roads, being below the surface of the ground, though open to the light and air, are not as pleasant as they would be if they were not so confined. A lady in her carriage, or a gentleman on horseback or on foot, making calls in the side of the city opposite to where they live; a physician called suddenly to visit a patient; a patient needing suddenly to summon his physician; boys and girls going to school or to college; —it will be allowed that in such cases as these a better means of communication than that afforded by the traffic-road ought to be provided, but, it seems to us, that these are not the only cases which need to be considered. We dare say that men of the large humanity of the designers of this Park did not forget the equal claim of those who have humbler errands. The washerwoman going home with her basket of snow after a hard day's work over tub or ironing-table; the sewing-girl shut up since early morning in a crowded room with the click of her sewing-machine in her ear for the oriole's song; the teacher fagged with disciplining those boys whom Plato declared to be the most ferocious of wild beasts;—all these, and more beside, need after their labors the rest of a quiet walk with grass and trees and sky, to make up for something of what has been lost in the wear and tear of the day. For such as these the easy communication by flowing diagonals from the Eighth Avenue and Fifty-ninth Street to Seventy-second and Seventy-ninth streets on the Fifth Avenue; from the entrance at the Fifth Avenue and Fifty-ninth Street to Seventy-second Street; and the more direct roads that we have already mentioned at Seventy-second, Ninety-sixth, and One Hundred and Second streets—were surely designed, and offer a most useful preparation for the day's labor, and a most welcome rest after it is over.

As we have reached the neighborhood of the Terrace, we may as well visit it now as leave it till our return. Yet the Terrace can only be thoroughly seen and enjoyed by those who are on foot, and as it is useless for us to attempt a regular and uninterrupted progress through the Park in this imaginary visit of ours, we will place ourselves again at the southern end of the Mall and approach the Terrace through this overarching green alley, of which it is the carefully designed terminus.

The two divisions of the Park which we have called "the upper" and the "lower," although artificially separated by the great

THE TERRACE FROM THE NORTH.

Reservoirs of the Croton Aqueduct, are, nevertheless, clearly defined by their natural differences. That portion of the ground north of the Reservoirs is distinguished by the freer sweep and greater variety of its horizon lines, and by the much more beautiful and interesting character of the landscape, not merely in the Park itself, but of the surrounding country, which can be commanded from its most elevated points. This upper park is much better suited to be dealt with by the landscape gardener, who produces his most legitimate effects with trees and grass and flowers, with rocks and water, and who relies as little as possible upon buildings of any kind. The lower park, on the contrary, is almost entirely artificial in its construction, and depends greatly for its attractiveness on artificial beauties. Not to trouble the reader with a too scientific statement, we will say in a word that the rocky ridge, on the edge of which New York island lies, comes to the surface at about Thirtieth Street, and is to be met with, chiefly on the western side, from that point to Manhattanville. From this ridge to the Hudson is three-quarters of a mile, and to the East River nearly a mile. On the eastern slope the Central Park is placed, and all the water, therefore, that either falls in rain, or flows from springs, finds its way naturally into the East River. The tract, however, is by no means a uniform slope; it is divided transversely by four irregular ridges, with their corresponding valleys, the chief of these ridges crossing the Park somewhat diagonally, and thus making the greatest elevation in the central, westerly, and northwesterly portions. But there are very few places in the whole extent of the Park where rock is not to be met with; with the exception of two tracts—partly boggy and partly meadow—of ten acres, or thereabouts, each, the report tells us that there is not an acre in the lower park, and nearly the same may be said of the upper park, where a crowbar could, originally, have been thrust its length into the ground without striking rock; and even where the gneiss was not visible to the eye (and for the most part it lay bare to the sun with neither mould, nor weeds, nor even moss upon it), it was found to be within from two inches to three feet of the surface for long distances together. This was the condition of the Park when Messrs. Olmsted and Vaux began operations, and it may well be imagined that it was no easy task to prepare this barren waste for beauty. Let us glance for a moment at the topography of this lower park. We find in it two lateral valleys, one running from about Sixty-fourth Street to the Fifth Avenue angle ; the waters that drained this depression have been gathered into the Pond, which we have already described. The second valley extended from Seventy-seventh Street and Eighth Avenue to Seventy-fourth Street and Fifth Avenue. The division between these two valleys was a rocky plateau covered with a moderately thick soil, but the remainder of the lower park was made up of low hills and hillocks, the rock of which they were composed everywhere cropping out boldly in large, smooth, flattish masses, washed bare of soil. Of this second valley, the northern side was an irregular rocky hill-side, crowned most inartistically by the walls of the old Reservoir, and this was easily in sight from every eminence in the lower park. As nature had refused to do any thing whatever for this region, had, indeed, done every thing to make it a sheet of white paper for man to write what he could upon, there was absolutely nothing to be done, but to bring in all the aids of art and create the attractions which nature had failed to furnish out of her own treasury. The plan was a simple one, but it was well calculated to produce the maximum of effect. The walk we have already described—the Mall—crosses the central plateau between the two depressions, diagonally, but in a direction nearly north and south. It is planted along its whole length with a double row of American elms, set so as to leave entirely clear the walk proper, of thirty-five feet in width. In the original design there was no entrance to the Mall from the sides, but at present two walks cross it, connecting the foot-paths that run parallel with it on either side. Near the upper end we come to the Music-stand, a remarkably pretty structure, where, twice a week, a first-rate band performs, and makes an attraction which, on a fine day, draws immense crowds. The Music-stand itself is decorated with colors and gilding after a design by Mr. Jacob Wrey Mould, a gentleman to whom, as we shall presently see,

THE MUSIC-STAND.

the public is indebted for almost all the decorative work in the Park, and without whose help the Terrace, especially, could hardly have become the attraction it has proved. Just beyond the Music-stand we reach the end of the Mall, which opens upon an ample rectangle of gravel, ornamented with two fountains, with gilded bird-cages, and with two extremely pretty drinking-basins. On music-days when the sun is oppressive, this square is covered with a light awning, and set with benches, where ladies and children gather and eat creams and ices to the "Minuet" in Don Juan, or "Le sabre de mon père."

On the opposite side of this pretty *plaza* an elegant screen of Albert freestone separates it from the carriage-road, to which access is given, however, by two openings, one at each side, so that persons can either leave their carriages to walk in the Mall and listen to the music, or can take them again after the entertainment is

over.   This carriage-road, as will be seen by the Plan, runs along
the edge of the second of the two valleys which we have mentioned

TERRACE—LOOKING SOUTH.

as dividing the lower park ; and the lake which lies at the bottom
of this depression—for " valley," perhaps, is too high-sounding a
name—is at present the chief point of interest in the whole Park,
though it was originally intended only as a centre of attraction for
the southern portion.   As on music-days, and it is hoped that, before long, every day will be a music-day, a great number of people
assemble at this point, in the Mall and on the plaza, on foot, and,
in the broad drive, in carriages and on horseback—it was found
necessary to provide a means of reaching the lower level of the lake
without the necessity of crossing the road, which, especially for
timid women and for children, would almost always be dangerous.
Between the two openings in the stone-screen a wide flight of steps
leads down from the plaza to a broad and well-lighted passage giving upon the Terrace and the Lake.

We have already spoken of the theory on which the drives,
rides, and walks in the Park are arranged—the theory that every

person who comes here shall be enabled to enjoy his visit in his own way; that those in carriages shall not be obliged to look out

STAIRS LEADING TO THE LAKE—TERRACE.

for the safety of persons on foot; that horsemen shall be free to canter, to gallop, or to trot, without the fear of meeting either carriages or pedestrians; and that those who come for a walk, whether it be a meditative stroll or a brisk "constitutional," shall not be run over by Jehus, or knocked down by any fiery Pegasus.* Horsemen may, if they choose, ride upon the carriage-roads, but pedestrians who take either the drives or the rides do so at their own risk. Children, however, are not permitted to leave the walks, and, by keeping to these, a muscular infant might toddle from one end of the Park to the other, and run no danger whatever.

* There is no law of the Park that forbids to turn and wind the fiery Pegasus, and witch the world with wondrous horsemanship, if it can be done; but Jehu is not allowed to try his skill. Not only is it forbidden to drive beyond a certain moderate rate, but the roads are intentionally so laid out as to make racing impossible.

It was for the purpose of carrying the foot-walk under the car-riage-road at this particular point that the elaborate architecture of the Terrace was designed. It is at present incomplete, and indeed it must be many years before the design, as it exists on paper, can be fully carried out, because it includes full-length statues, as also busts, of distinguished Americans, which it is intended to place upon the large pedestals that are now covered with temporary ornamental caps. The Commissioners have done wisely in mak-ing no attempt whatever as yet to procure statues for these places, and it ought not to be done until there is ample means to secure the best work possible in America. First-rate statues are as yet hardly to be got for money here, though we cordially believe that they will be produced in good time; but until they can be had it is best to wait, for a second-rate statue is like a tolerable egg—it is not to be endured. If one statue is found fit to be placed upon the Terrace in a generation, we shall think we are getting on very well indeed. But so long as the pedestals want their heroes, so long the Terrace will be incomplete, and people will be half-justified in saying that it looks squat. This, how-ever, is a difficulty which it was not possible for the architects to avoid. They probably never expected nor intended that the Park would be completed in a single decade, nor in two. Indeed, until every tree upon it is fully grown, the effect they had in view at the beginning cannot be realized.

We must consider the Terrace, then, as an incomplete archi-tectural composition, and admire the beauty and variety of its decoration without troubling ourselves at the absence of what we should be very sorry to see supplied, unless it enhanced and crowned those ornaments which are intended to be, finally, not principal but subsidiary. And in passing down the broad and elegant stairs that lead to the lower level, we wish to call the visitors' attention to the panels of the railing which surround the well of the staircase. It will be observed that no two of all these many panels are alike, but their beauty and ingenuity are much more worthy of admiration than their mere variety. This part of the Terrace was first completed—this and the stone screen-work on the opposite side of the road. On the staircase leading from the carriage-drive to the lower terrace the carving of the rails and posts with their connecting ramps was executed later; much of it has been only lately finished, and much remains to do. The earlier work is of a more conventional character than the later, although it is all based on the forms of vegetation, but the decoration of the two great staircases on the north is almost purely naturalistic, being symbolic of the four seasons. The main design of the Terrace stone-work is due to Mr. Calvert Vaux, but the credit of the entire decoration is given by him to his able assistant, Mr. Mould. Of this gentleman we have before spoken; we need not say that he is a man of remarkable genius, for his name is by this time widely known, but his connection with the architecture of the Park has not been sufficiently recognized. The truth is that Mr. Mould, who for a long time served as simply an assistant to the architect-in-chief, Mr. Olmsted, and to the consulting architect, Mr. Vaux, has proved himself worthy of the equal mention which, after the lapse of nearly ten years, the Commissioners have at length awarded him in the last report, where he is no longer styled an assistant, but a principal.

Mr. Mould is an Englishman by birth and education. Having graduated both at the school and the college of King's College, London, he was entered as an articled pupil in the office of Owen Jones, where he remained from 1840 to 1848. While studying under the direction of this accomplished artist, Mr. Mould transferred to stone the whole of the second volume of Owen Jones's great work on the Alhambra—the Detail volume—and also executed wholly the well-known Gray's Elegy Illuminated, and the illustrations and illuminations of the Book of Common Prayer, published by John Murray. While he was getting steadiness of hand, and educating his eye in color under the guidance of Owen

JACOB WREY MOULD.

Jones, he was not so thoroughly taught in construction, for this was never a strong point with his master. In 1848, however, Mr. Mould became the first assistant to Mr. Lewis Vulliamy, Sir Robert Smirke's first pupil, and author of a well-known work on Greek Ornament. Mr. Vulliamy being an excellent constructionist, his new assistant had now the opportunity he had so long desired, to supplement his knowledge of decorative art with skill in more purely architectural studies. And he was soon brought into the thick of a most searching practical experience. Mr. Vulliamy received the commission from Mr. Holford, an English gentleman, to build a mansion for him on the site of Dorchester House. This was one of the most splendid commissions that has been given by a private person to any architect of our time. But, scarcely had work been begun on the plans, when Mr. Vulliamy, at the age of seventy, slipped on the ice at Highgate, and sustained a severe injury that confined him to his house for four years. During that time Mr. Mould had entire control of the office, and built Holford House. Its splendor may be imagined from one single item. Two grand staircases were designed for it by Mr. Mould, of which, one was estimated at £32,000, and the other at £56,000. Mr. Holford chose the more costly, which was built, and stands to-day the most beautiful work of its kind in Europe. Mr. Mould came to this country in 1852. Shortly after his arrival in New York, and after he had proved his ability in the erection of several important structures, he was invited to assist Mr. Vaux in the architectural department of the Park, where he has ever since been fully employed. His graceful and unwearied hand is seen in many places, and, we hope, will be seen in many more; but his principal performance in the Park has, thus far, been the Terrace, the general design of which is by Mr. Vaux, but all the details have been left to Mr. Mould. His work is remarkable for its variety and its suggestiveness. He combines a strong feeling for color with an equal enjoyment of form, and he has such delight in his art that it is far easier for him to make every fresh design an entirely new one, than to copy something he has made before. It was a fortunate day for the public when Mr. Vaux made his acquaintance, and with that quick appreciation of excellence which distinguishes him, called him to his assistance.

Descending the stairs that lead from the *Plaza* to the lower terrace we find ourselves in a large and delightfully cool hall which has been constructed under the carriage-road. Its decoration is not yet completed, but enough is finished to show how

rich, and yet how elegant, will be the final effect. The walls
are of Albert freestone, with large circular-headed niches,

STONE SCREEN DIVIDING PLAZA FROM CARRIAGE ROAD.

designed to be filled in with elaborate arabesque patterns in
encaustic tiles. The whole floor is laid with Minton's tiles, and
the ceiling is composed of richly gilded iron beams, enclosing
large squares of colored tiles, this being the first time, we believe, that tiles have been used here for ceiling decoration. It
was for a long time a problem how to fix them securely beyond
the peradventure of a fall, perhaps upon some luckless pate. By
a very ingenious, but very simple, device, the desired safety has
been secured, and the whole ceiling is being covered in the following manner:—In the first place all the tiles used in the Terrace
were first designed by Mr. Mould, and the drawings sent over
and executed at Minton's works in England. As ordinarily manufactured, the tiles have a number of holes sunk in the under
side and certain flattish depressions beside crossing the surface

in squares, these holes and depressions being for the purpose of
binding the tile to the cement which is forced into the body of
the tile by pressure, and, when dry, holds it very securely. In
this way all the tiles used in the Terrace flooring and wall work
are constructed, but something more was needed in the tiles made
for the ceiling. In the middle of the back of each of these a
narrow slot is sunk, into which a brass key with a projecting
end fits, and is secured by a turn. The hole is then filled up
with cement, and the removal of the key is impossible, except
by using considerable force. The tiles having been all prepared
in this way, a plate of wrought iron, fitted into a frame, is elevated
by a screw-jack to the top of an iron scaffolding, placed under
one of the squares formed by the intersection of the iron beams
of the ceiling. This plate is exactly the size of the square under
which it now lies. It is pierced with as many holes as there are
tiles to be laid upon it, and the projecting ends of the brass keys
we have mentioned fit easily into these holes, and are secured
by brass nuts screwed upon the opposite side. When the pattern
is complete, and each tile firmly fixed in its place, the great iron
plate is reversed by a simple machinery and elevated to its place
in the ceiling, where it is held fast to the beams by strong screws.
So neatly is the work done, that, to all appearances, the tiles are
laid upon the ceiling as they are laid upon the floor.

All the stone-work of this interior is beautifully carved, though
nowhere in excess, but to one who enjoys such things it is a
pleasure to study the variety of design, no two caps or pilasters
being alike.

And here let it be said that it is not the artist nor the lover
of art alone, to whose pleasure and instruction it has been sought
to minister in the construction of the Terrace, and, indeed of
every material construction in the Park. It certainly has not
been from any mere desire to spend money, or to make a display, that the Commissioners have seconded the architects in

their determination to have all the mechanical work required on the Park done in the very best possible way without stinting, though by no means without counting the cost. But it has been felt that, even if every great public work were not most cheaply done when it is done most thoroughly well, here was, beside, an opportunity to teach many lessons to American mechanics in a quiet and unpretending way. On the Park our people have had the advantage of seeing the whole operation of building these admirable roads, which have never thus far been even approached in thoroughness of construction and fitness for their several purposes, on this side of the water, and, probably,

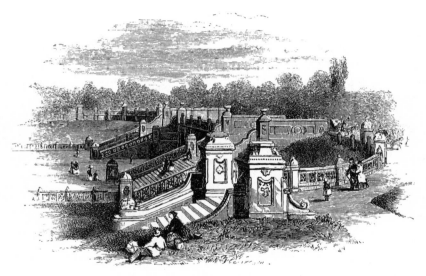

STAIRS FROM CARRIAGE-ROAD TO LOWER TERRACE.

have never been surpassed anywhere. Here, also, has been to study from the beginning the best masonry that the skill of our own and of foreign workmen can produce; and all over the Park, by the ingenious management and prudent forethought of the superintendent, engineers, and architects, backed by the unfailing zeal and constant watchfulness of the Comptroller and Treasurer,

Andrew H. Green, Esq., the lesson has been taught what admirable results flow from faithful work, from a large economy, and from strict adherence to plans elaborated with care, and proved wise by every year's added experience.

On leaving the Hall we come out upon the lower terrace between the two great stairs that descend to it from the carriage-road. These staircases have been designed with a view to receive a great deal of ornamented sculpture, and much of it has already been executed. There are, of course, two balustrades with their posts and ramps to each of the two staircases, and the four have been made emblematic of the seasons. On the newel posts of the balustrades are carved on three sides the animals and fruits that belong to the several seasons—bees, birds, butterflies, grapes, and berries. The balustrades themselves are formed of panels with open borders, each panel being filled with a flower or fruit in the balustrades belonging to Spring, Summer, and Autumn, while those of Winter are prettily designed with the leaves and cones of evergreen, and in one of them is a pair of skates. All these panels are designed with the idea of keeping as close to nature as possible, conventionalizing the objects no more than has been necessary to bring them into the squares of the panels. The freest and most elaborate sculpture has been reserved for the ramps which take the place of balustrades between the first landing and the posts at the head of the stairs. The designs for these ramps are composed of flowing scrolls, formed by the branches of flowering plants, among which birds hover, alight, and play. On no public building in America has there yet been placed any sculpture so rich in design as this, or so exquisitely delicate in execution. It is not saying as much as it may seem to declare that all the sculpture on the walls of the new Houses of Parliament in London, is not worth, either for design or execution, these four ramps of the great stairs of the Terrace alone.

The lower terrace is a broad and cheerful plaza, giving access
to the Lake, communicating with the upper park by two foot-

FOUNTAIN ON LOWER TERRACE.

paths, and surrounded by a low wall or balustrade of carved
stone, along which runs a stone seat.   In the centre is a fountain
basin where it was originally intended to place a fountain designed by Miss Stebbins, but we are under the impression that
some change has taken place in the plans of the Commissioners
since the earlier reports were issued, in one of which—the eighth—
1864, an engraving was published of the design then determined
on.   At the northern side of this plaza is the station for the boats,
which now constitute one of the greatest attractions of the Park.
At either side is planted a lofty mast, from which depends a
standard; on one of these is embroidered the arms of the State,
and on the other the arms of the City—arms, so-called, though
of course they are not arms at all, but, as in the case of every
one of our States, and of all our cities, that pretend to them,
they are nothing but an incongruous and unartistic assemblage
of supposed emblems.   Such as they are, however, they are suspended from these elegantly ornamented masts, designed by Mr.
Mould.   The boats, which now number twenty-five, are fastened

to stakes in a long line at a short distance from the shore—the
keeper and his men occupying a small house on the water-edge

BANNER WITH THE ARMS OF THE STATE.

of the plaza. Although these boats are much used in the summer time, and the charge for a trip round the Lake is very small,
yet the report tells us that the contractor makes but a small sum
over his expenses. The boats are light and extremely pretty,
and their skilful management renders them perfectly safe, no

accident of any kind having happened in the use of them since the first two or three were placed on the Lake. Moored at the

BOAT HOUSE SOUTHWEST END OF LAKE.

eastern end of the Lake the visitor will see the Venetian gondola, presented to the Park, in 1862, by John A. C. Gray, Esq., formerly a commissioner. This is a real gondola and not a mere model, but it is not used, because Mr. Gray did not, at the same time, present the Commissioners with a Venetian gondolier to manage it! However, it looks sufficiently romantic, lying in all its low, black length upon this water hardly more ruffled than that of its native canals.

There are six landings where the boats can stop in the round trip, either to take up or to leave passengers. These landings are pretty structures, differing from one another in design, and are much frequented by the children, who sit in them to watch the swans and snow-white ducks who tamely come at a call. These swans form an unfailing delight to all young persons who visit the Park, and, indeed, are hardly less attractive to adults. In March, 1860, the City of Hamburgh through its consul to

BOAT HOUSE NEAR RAMBLE.

America, the late George Kunhardt, Esq., presented to the Board of Commissioners twelve of the beautiful swans for which that city has long been famous, offering at the same time to send them to this port free of all expense of transportation. Mr. R. M. Blatchford, at that time President of the Board, accepted the generous offer with the cordial thanks, not only of the Commissioners, but of the whole city; and a few weeks after the birds arrived in safety, in charge of a person sent out at the expense of the City of Hamburgh, with orders to remain until they were thoroughly domesticated; the owner of the steamer that brought him over having volunteered in the most praiseworthy spirit both to see that every thing in the power of her officers was done to insure the safe transportation of the swans, and to give a free passage home to the person having them in his charge. The birds were placed in the Lake, and for a time seemed to thrive, but in a few weeks nine of them had died, from apoplexy as was afterward proved, though at first it was suspected they had been poisoned.   The City of Hamburgh, as soon as it was informed through its consul of the death of the swans, presented the Commissioners with ten more; and R. W. Kennard, Esq., M. P., an esteemed Englishman, at that time living in New York, having informed the Worshipful Company of Vintners, and the Worshipful Company of Dyers, in the City of London, of the loss the citizens of New York had sustained, the former of these companies sent over twelve pairs, and the latter thirteen pairs, which reached America in safety and were placed upon the Lake.   In the report for 1862, it was announced that out of the original seventy-two twenty-eight had died, but since that time no additional deaths have been reported.   In the report for 1866 the number living is stated to be fifty-one, and in the last report, for 1867, the family counts sixty-four, showing

SWAN-REST ON LAKE.

an increase of twenty in five years, from which we may be encouraged to hope that these beautiful aristocrats have learned to accommodate themselves to our trying climate and to our democratic institutions.   Beside the white swans there are two trumpeter swans, who also have bred during the past year.   There is hardly a prettier sight to be seen than that of the female swan sailing about with her cygnets. The mother-bird assists the little blue-gray youngsters to mount her back, either by sinking so low in the water that they can climb up without difficulty, or else puts out one of her legs and makes a step for them. She then raises her wings, and arches back her neck, and thus makes a most comfortable shelter, impervious to the wind, in which the baby swans sit at their ease, or sleep, or look out upon the landscape, and, no doubt, think the most sweet and innocent thoughts.

The Park swans are very tame, and will come to the shore at a call to feed from any hand, although we believe the Commissioners do not like to have them fed in this way. As is well known, they are a greedy bird, and in their native habitat, or in ponds and rivers where they are domesticated, they

BOAT HOUSE NEAR OAK BRIDGE.

prey upon fish, and upon the eggs of fish, to such an extent as to make themselves the terror and the pest of enthusiastic anglers.

Wood, in his Natural History, quotes one of this class as burst-
ing into an agony of depreciation and throwing grammar to the
winds:—"There never was no manner of doubt about the dread-
ful mischief the swans do! They eats up the spawn of every
kind of fish till they have filled out their bags, and then on to
shore they goes, to sleep off their tuck out, and then at it again!"

As will be seen by the Plan, the Lake is of considerable size,
and extends very nearly across the Park. It is divided into two
parts, quite distinct in their character, by the Bow Bridge, as it
is called, a graceful structure of iron crossing the Lake at its
narrowest point by a span of eighty-seven feet and a third, and
at a height above the surface of nine feet and a half. With the
exception of the floor, which is, of course, of wood, it is made
entirely of wrought iron, resting on two abutments of stone, one
of the ends being placed upon cannon-balls, in order to allow
for the necessary expansion and contraction with heat and cold.

BOW BRIDGE FROM LAKE.

At the ends of the bridge, over the abutments, are placed iron
vases, which, in summer, are kept filled with flowering plants,
and it is not without reason that this is generally considered as

the handsomest of all the bridges in the Park. East of it the Lake is, perhaps, the more attractive. On one side is the Terrace, with its beautiful architecture, and gay crowds of happy, well-dressed people, its stream of carriages passing over the Terrace bridge, or stopping there to listen to the band, and along the shore the painted boats taking and discharging their loads. On the other is the hill-side called the Ramble, with its cheerful scenery in summer-time, and its blaze of colors in the autumn season. The portion of the Lake that lies beyond the Bow Bridge, to the west, is much larger, and presents less variety, but, to many, it will be more pleasing on that account. Here boys may fancy themselves at sea, and hope, by some lucky accident, to taste the terrors of shipwreck. Here there are some-times waves, and there is certainly an actual beach, where such waves as there may happen to be may dash themselves in break-ers. One of the main drives that starts from the gate-way at the corner of the Eighth Avenue and Fifty-ninth Street, skirts the

VIEW OF LAKE LOOKING SOUTH.

Lake on its western side, and, as it necessarily passes very near the boundary of the Park at this point, the aim in planting has been to shut off the Eighth Avenue and open up the Lake, and when the trees and shrubs are fully grown it will be found that this has been accomplished as far as it is possible to do it. The visitor will then find himself shut in, on one side by a belt of verdure, while on the other, his eye will be irresistibly attracted to the shining levels of the Lake, where, in the summer-time, the darting boats, and gliding swans, and groups of children on the shore, will make a bright and cheerful picture; and no less gay in winter will be the thronging crowds of skaters, from early morning till late at night, under the brilliant moon or the more brilliant calcium light.

The Lake is the principal field for skaters in the Park, although the Pond near Fifty-ninth Street is much used, and, in course of time, Harlem Lake, at the northern end, will become an equally favorite resort for citizens living in its neighborhood.* The teachings of Dr. Dio Lewis, and other earnest advocates of physical education, about ten years ago, had given a great impetus to open-air sports and athletic games in Boston and its vicinity, and a similar interest had been awakened in Philadelphia. In New York, Mrs. Plumb had established her excellent gymnasium for women, but our city was far less advantageously situated than Boston for sports and exercises that required ample out-of-door space for their full enjoyment. The exercise was good, but it failed of its full effect in restoring or maintaining health when it had to be taken in the house. Both Boston and Philadelphia had the great advantage over New York, of possessing,

---

* The number of days in which there was skating in 1861–62....50

"	"	"	"	1864–65....50
"	"	"	"	1866–67....39
"	"	"	"	1859–60....36
"	"	"	"	1865–66....28
"	"	"	"	1860–61....27
"	"	"	"	1863–64....24
"	"	"	"	1858–59....19
"	"	"	"	1862–63.... 6

either within their boundaries, or in their immediate vicinity, abundant room for any exercise that might be in fashion. Boston Common had, for many years, given the city boys a central and convenient place for play with sleds, and the Frog-Pond, with the excellent ponds within easy access of the city, had enabled everybody who wished it to get a taste of skating dur-

BOW BRIDGE FROM BEACH.

ing the season; while, in Philadelphia, the Schuylkill afforded an incomparable field for this latter exercise, of which hundreds had availed themselves every winter for many years, and, later, as the sport became more fashionable, and skaters counted by thousands rather than by hundreds, the river was ready with room and to spare for all who chose to come.

But New York had no place near or far-off where open-air exercise could be obtained, and, as for skating, it had become an almost forgotten art. That it should be utterly forgotten was, of course, not to be believed, because skating must be supposed to be a principle in Dutch blood, and experience has since proved that in this instance, as in many others, nature, although driven out with a fork, returns in full force at the first opportunity.   When the New York boys and girls heard of the zeal with which their brothers and sisters in Boston and Philadelphia were flying over the face of the earth on skates,

LAKE VIEW.

they were moved with envy and emulation, and in default of frozen lakes and rivers, they fastened skates with wheels instead of sharpened steel to their feet, and careered over the flagged sidewalks and over parlor floors, with the laudable determination to en-joy skating in imagination if they could not in reality. On the whole, it resembled the real thing about as nearly as the marchioness's orange-peel and water did wine. "If you shut your eyes very tight," said that young person to Mr. Dick Swiveller, "and make believe very hard, you really would almost think it was wine."   And perhaps young New York might have gone on making believe very hard that skating on wheels was as good as skating on skates, if the Commissioners had not asked them all to come up to the Park and try the real thing.

In their tenth report (1866), the Commissioners claim, and, no doubt, rightly, that the facilities for skating so freely offered by the Central Park, have set the fashion to New York and all the neighboring region.   There had always been, every win-ter, more or less ice accessible to the rougher part of the popula-tion, and even to more fastidious people, who were willing to go in search of it.   But there was nowhere to be found ice that was kept in good condition for skating the whole season through, that was cleared of new-fallen snow, and flooded after a thaw, or after the feet of hundreds had destroyed its surface. No private person or company had yet been found willing to risk the money which such an enterprise would call for, and, indeed, no one had even suggested that such an enterprise was called for, or was even possible. But no sooner had the first winter's trial at the Central Park proved the perfect feasibility of the undertaking than private subscription ponds were formed in every direction. In the city they were mostly in the neighborhood of the Park, and were made by flooding the sunken lots which so abound in that region. These were then boarded up in order to prevent indiscriminate access, and rough buildings were put up near the entrance, to accommodate the visitors, who were all either subscribers for the season, or paid a fee for each admission. At night these private ponds, like those of the Central Park, were illuminated by calcium lights, and they were sometimes supplied with music, which the Park was not. They drew off, of course, a great many visitors from the Park skating grounds, then chiefly of the wealthy, and many ladies and young children; but this was by no means undesirable, since the skating grounds of the Park have always been, from the beginning, overcrowded. Nor were these small city ponds the only ones that were established to meet the new-found want. In Brooklyn, in Hoboken, along the line of the Harlem and New Haven Railroads, ponds were advertised, and vied with one another in the attractions they held out to skaters. Masquerades were held upon the ice; concerts were given; fireworks were displayed; and for a time there was an active competition. But, as will be seen by the table, our changeable climate makes the speculation a too uncertain one to be relied upon for making money. In nine years it will be seen that the number of skating days has varied all the way from six to fifty, and there were only two years in the nine when there have been so many as fifty.

Of course this uncertainty makes the risk too great to be run with impunity, and only persons owning, or having right in, large natural ponds can afford to continue these enterprises. Beside, the sunken lots are rapidly being built up, and it will not be long before they will disappear altogether. With the Park skating grounds it is quite different. It requires no additional staff of workmen to keep the ice in condition through the season, nor any addition to the police force to maintain order. The ponds are there, and the arrangements for flooding them are simple and always on hand, and whatever expense—never very great—is incurred to provide skating, is for the public service, and makes an item in the annual budget. Nor can the pleasure that is given to so many thousands, and the health and strength they gain, be reckoned in money.

While we are upon this subject it may be worth while to notice the fact, that with the increased opportunities for skating has come a steady improvement in the skates that are yearly offered for sale. Skaters are now as much exercised over the shape and material of their instrument as horseback riders are over their saddles, and cricket-players over their bats and balls. If a countryman should appear to-day upon the ground, proud in the possession of a pair of fine old skates, inherited from his grandfather, with their double-gutters, multiplied straps, and ends curling up over the instep like the proboscis of some gigantic butterfly, we shudder to think of the persecution of inquisitive commentary to which he would subject himself. The little boys who officiate as skate-strappers would sit in awful judgment upon him. The ladies would pierce him through and through with glances of playful scorn, and he would learn by sad experience how soon the fashion of this world passeth away.

The northern end of the western division of the Lake is reserved for the use of ladies who come to skate, although they are free to go anywhere they may please. But it was thought best to reserve a place for the more timid and delicate ones, and for those, also, who are just beginning to practise. The

LADIES' SKATING POND.

Ladies' Pond is much frequented, but the men are by no means on that account left to the enjoyment of the rest of the Lake in selfish exclusiveness. Here, as in so many departments of our modern social life, woman competes with man on ground in which he had indulged the absurd fancy that he was without a rival, and, in spite of all his efforts, either carries off the palm or fairly divides the victory.

Our Scotch fellow-citizens too have found a use for the Lake in winter, and the curling club have introduced here their manly and graceful national game. Some of our readers may remember Mr. J. G. Brown's capital portrait picture of the members of this club, called "Curling, Central Park," in the Academy exhibition of 1863.

The carriage-road that skirts the western side of the Lake crosses, near Seventy-seventh Street, a narrow strait leading from the main water into a small pond close to the Eighth Avenue.

CURLING.

The bridge by which the drive is carried over this connecting stream is called the Balcony Bridge, from the two projecting balconies with stone seats, formed by corbelling out the piers. These are pleasant places in which to sit and overlook the Lake, and, architecturally, this bridge is one of the handsomest in the Park. One of our cuts shows the view looking toward Balcony Bridge from the beach; the one a little farther on shows the bridge from the western side, which has no balconies, since the view on that side is so limited as to make them hardly necessary.

Returning to the Terrace for a fresh start, we ascend the steps at the right hand from the lower plaza to the upper, and stop for a moment to look at the bronze statue of the tigress which has been recently presented to the Park by a few American gentlemen temporarily residing in Europe. The statue will be found on a little slope west of the Terrace and very near it.

In ascending to it we may notice at the right hand the two specimens of the "Great Tree" of California (*sequoia gigantea*), both of which appear to be thriving well; and near the summit

BALCONY BRIDGE.

of the knoll are two well-grown specimens of the Japanese sacred tree, the Ginkgo, or maiden-hair (*salisburia adiantifolia*), which has been a rare tree in this country until within a very few years. For a long time the only specimens in this part of America were the original plants at The Woodlands, formerly the seat of Alexander Hamilton, Esq., near Philadelphia, by whom it was first introduced into this country, in 1784; those in the old Bartram Garden, near Philadelphia; one that stood on Boston Common, and still stands there, if the climate have not proved too severe for it; and, finally, a specimen at Pierce's Park, near Westchester, Pennsylvania. It has long been a puzzle to botanists, who have been unable to classify it, but Mr. Josiah Hoopes, in his recently published and very valuable "Book of Evergreens," places it among the Coniferæ on the strength of its fruit, which he says settles the question. It is a very rapid growing tree, is exceedingly elegant in its shape and in its foliage, and when these specimens in the Park once assume a sufficient size to attract general attention, we shall hope to see the Ginkgo become as familiar a denizen of our gardens as are so many plants and trees of China and Japan.

BALCONY BRIDGE FROM THE BEACH.

It has been several times proposed to establish in the Park an Arboretum, or a Botanical Garden, and the notion is not a bad one, or would not be, if the Park were two or three times as large as it is. But, to our thinking, it is quite as agreeable a way of studying the different varieties of plants, and trees, and flowers, to find them scattered over the whole Park, as it would be to have them planted more scientifically in rows and squares, as for convenience of classification and reference they must be in a botanic garden. For our part, we like to come upon these pretty strangers unawares; to catch them, as it were, off their guard, rather than to go through the formalities of an introduction—

"in arbors clipt and cut,
And alleys, faded places.
By squares of tropic summer shut
And warmed in crystal cases."

The limits of the Park are, at best, so narrow that it seems a pity to make them seem still more contracted by dividing the space into districts or departments, especially into such formal ones as all strictly scientific collections make necessary. Rather, in this particular case, make the whole Park a botanical garden, giving each plant as far as possible, its native habitat and surroundings, and fixing near it, in a quiet, informal way, a label with its name. The scientific man and the poet can then enjoy it, each in his own way.

On the summit of the slight eminence to which we have ascended, chatting about trees, we find the bronze statue of the tigress bringing food to her cubs, which we came to see. It is the production of the celebrated Auguste Caine, and was cast in bronze by the equally distinguished F. Barbadienne, whose magnificent enamels were without a rival in the recent Exposition, at Paris. This bronze was presented to the Park in 1867, in a letter to A. H. Greene, Esq., the Comptroller, by twelve gentlemen, citizens of New York. It is six feet high and seven and half feet in length, and stands, at present, upon a temporary pedestal of wood. We cannot agree with those who think such figures as this of the Tigress, and that of the Eagles bringing their prey to their young, particularly suitable to the Park. They are, both of them, fine and spirited works of their kind, but they are much better suited to a zoological garden than to a place like the Park, for the ideas they inspire do not belong to the tranquil, rural beauty of the Park scenery. They are not, to our thinking, a whit more appropriate than the funeral monuments would be which the Commissioners so wisely and absolutely refuse to admit. Indeed,

if it were not for the sake of establishing a dangerous precedent, it might be far less objectionable to admit some funeral
monuments that one might name than to give room to these

THE TIGRESS.

savage subjects. There have been glorious deaths—fit endings
to noble lives—whose records could only inspire high and cheerful thoughts, fitted to any scene in nature, however beautiful or
grand; but sculpture of the class to which the pieces we have
mentioned belong, has little that is elevating in its tendency.
They are simply records of carnage and rapine, and however
masterly the execution, or however profound the scientific observation they display, they are apart from the purpose of noble
art, whose aim is to lift the spirit of man to a higher region and
feed him with grander thoughts.

There is no one among the many difficult subjects almost daily presented to the Park authorities for consideration, more difficult than the limit to be placed to the admission of sculpture into the Park. To persons who have not given much thought to the matter it may seem that the easiest, and also the wisest, thing the Commissioners could do, would be to take every piece of statuary that is offered them, that has any merit whatever, and find a place for it somewhere in the Park. But to this the Commissioners very properly, as it appears to us, demur. In the first place, they do not want any statuary at all, unless it is the best that can be produced. Looking upon the Park as they do, not merely as a place of amusement, but as a place of education, they have always considered it a matter of conscience to exclude every thing that falls short of the standard they have proposed to themselves. It may be very difficult to get good statuary; they may have to wait a long time for it; but they cannot see in either of these suppositions any argument for permitting the precedent of placing second-rate or indifferent works of art in the Park until the good works shall arrive. The Commissioners were probably not much delighted at the prospect of having a statue of Shakspeare in the Park, for it was extremely unlikely that a good one could be procured. Probably no living sculptor could have succeeded better—we do not know one who could have succeeded so well—as Mr. Ward has done, but the difficulty of the task is so immeasurable that to have succeeded at all is something both the artist and the public must be congratulated upon. Even such small matters as the bust of Schiller and the Bronze Eagles (although the latter is, as we have said, not inappropriate to the zoological garden), must have placed the Commissioners in something of a dilemma. On the one hand, they could not, without offence, decline the gifts—it seems to be a settled principle to accept the smallest favors, from the skeleton of a negro to a copper medal advertising a soda-fountain manufacturer—and on the other, they could not but feel that the gifts themselves were not particularly desirable possessions.   In time it is to be hoped that the pride

BUST OF SCHILLER.

of the Germans in their second great national poet will lead them to replace the present very unsatisfactory memorial of him with a worthy statue; and in time it will also be easy to remove the spirited bronze of the "Eagles Devouring their Prey" to a more suitable place in the Zoological Garden, but it must be evident that the Commissioners cannot be always accepting costly, if not valuable gifts, which they are obliged to get rid of, or to dispose of in some way, however inconvenient. They are, therefore, obliged to be very chary in accepting gifts, by no means

ready to encourage them, and to maintain an independent atti-
tude to those who offer them. For it is a trait observed in all
persons who come to the Park with gifts in their hands that,
with rare exceptions, they consider themselves as placing, not
the Park alone, but the whole body of citizens, under great
obligations, and they think the least that can be done to show
a proper sense of that obligation is, to give their special gifts
the most conspicuous place that can be selected. These demands have, no doubt, often placed the Commissioners in a
position of great difficulty, and yet they are obliged to meet
the responsibility, and settle the matter in the best way they
can, with an eye solely to the interests of the Park. Thus far
there has not been a single piece of statuary presented to the
Park and placed in it that it is at all desirable to have there. The
statue of Commerce, presented in 1865, by Stephen B. Guion,
Esq., a native of New York long resident in Liverpool, is a
mere commonplace emblematic figure, such as are all the time
being produced in French studios, but which have very little
meaning or interest for the great mass of people, and for artists
none at all of either. Yet, what are the Commissioners to do?
A much respected gentleman, animated by a praiseworthy desire
to do something for the adornment of his native city, orders this
statue from Fesquet—a clever French statuary—and in the quiet-
est, most modest way possible, presents it to the Park, without
imposing any conditions, without asking for any particular site,
without even attaching his name to the gift. It certainly is very
much to be wished that the respected donor had given us something else; that he had ordered, for instance, Quincy Ward to
put his Indian Hunter into bronze, or had given a commission
to Story, or to Brown, or to Launt Thompson; but, as he did
not do any of these things, we must make the most of the gift
he has presented. It has accordingly been placed near the entrance at the southwestern angle of the Park—Eighth Avenue

and Fifty-ninth Street—where will one day be the Merchants' Gate, and among the emblems that will find an appropriate place in the architecture of this gate, perhaps the statue of Commerce

STATUE OF COMMERCE.

may occupy a conspicuous position. Just at present it stands entirely unrelated to any thing that surrounds it, and no statue so situated can possibly be fairly judged.

To the bronze figure of the Tigress we have already alluded. It is undoubtedly a work of merit in its way, belonging to a class of sculpture far removed from the heroic or the ideal, and only calculated to give a transient and not elevated pleasure.

With the purpose the architects have had in view in the construction of the Terrace it would not have been possible, without inconsistency, to give this statue a conspicuous place in relation to the Terrace, and indeed it is not easy to see whereabouts in the Park it can be conspicuously placed at all. It has, therefore, been set up in a secluded spot, shut off from general observation by a screen of trees, and while placed so that whoever chooses to seek it can see thoroughly well all that there is of it, it does not in the least interfere with the artistic arrangement of the Terrace and its surroundings. But its proper place is not here at all; it is, as we have said, in the Zoological Garden, of which it would make a very attractive and appropriate ornament.

It will be seen, then, that the whole subject of sculpture in the Park is beset with difficulties, and that the Commissioners have more than any mere personal interests, whether of their own or of other people, to consult. For, apart from the question of good or bad sculpture, is the problem how to limit its introduction to such a point that it shall not detract from the apparent size of the Park; a most serious consideration. Many of our readers must have had the opportunity of observing how quickly the apparent size of a garden is reduced by the introduction of statuary, which it was at one time the fashion to use much more freely than has been done since the "natural style" of gardening came into vogue. Not only is the area of the garden or lawn so ornamented diminished to the eye, but walks and roads along which statuary is placed are visibly shortened. Both these facts are no less facts for being optical delusions, which are the result of a well-known natural law. They are delusions constantly taken into account in decorative design, and cannot safely be neglected. Their bearing on the question of the Park is plain. The area of the Park, however large it may sound when stated to the ear, or however it may seem on paper, is in proportion to the population that is to use it, by no means so large as it seems to the superficial observer. And this process must continue; the Park growing sensibly smaller and smaller with every conspicuous object that is placed in it giving the eye a means of measurement, until, at length, its real dimensions cannot any longer be concealed. Any visitor to the Park who chooses to observe, can see this process going on everywhere within its limits. Every summer-house that is built on rising ground, the new Spa, the ugly gate-houses of the Reservoir—another feat in ornamental architecture of our friends, the engineers—the Children's Shelter, the Belvidere that is to be—each of these structures draws the eye to itself from a distance, and suggests a limit, a bound. This would be all very well if the distances in the Park were really grand, if calling attention to a limit was equivalent to saying, "see, how far!" But when the unfortunate shape of the Park is considered, its narrowness, which no amount of planting, however judiciously done, can ever hope to make entirely forgotten; its pronounced division into two parts, a defect only to be made the best of, not to be got rid of; it will be seen that the one thing to be avoided, is the calling attention to limits which can only mean, "see, how near!" And when we have thoroughly understood the serious nature of the problem thus presented to the Commissioners, we shall appreciate the force of their objection to multiplying statues, and not merely statues, but objects of any kind that do not serve some necessary purpose, or that do not tend to assist, but rather interfere with, their plans for the decoration of the Park on the highest artistic principles.

We imagine that under any circumstances, even if the Park were a great deal larger than it is, the truest taste would dictate that there should be as few artificial objects in it as possible. The charm of the Park ought to consist chiefly in its broad stretches of green grass, its lakes, and pools, and streams, its fine trees, its shrubs and abundant flowers, and the sky that overarches and encloses all. Those who are all the week "in populous city pent," see in their daily walks enough architecture and enough statuary; enough, and more than enough, of all that is artificial, and far too little of natural beauty. The best architecture and, indeed, the best art of whatever kind, can never be fully appreciated or enjoyed by those who have no familiarity with nature. The Park is only a blessing and a means of education, in proportion as it gives an opportunity to men, women, and children to become unconsciously familiar with the large traits of earth and sky. And no substantial good is done by crowding the prospect with what are called works of art. For if it be true, as our poet has sung,—

—"no mountain can
Measure with a perfect man,"

it is also true that no material work of man can measure with a mountain; nature gives us the scale by which to gauge every creation of art. And we are sure that a great deal of the petty and narrow criticism of the day would be enlarged, grow higher and broader, if it were written under the sky rather than under a roof. And our art would grow also, if both those who produce it, and those for whom it is produced, lived in greater familiarity with nature. The great danger is, lest the Park should come to be looked upon merely as a place wherein are collected a large number of curious and rare, or pretty things, which would, it is true, be a recommendation to a museum, or to a garden of plants or animals, but is not proper to a park. A park is a place of rest and recreation for mind and body; and while nature soothes and tranquillizes the mind, and thus gives the body that repose it needs, a number of petty objects, merely curious or pleasing, distracts the thoughts and frets the nerves. Of course, in a large public place, many tastes must be considered, and many wants ministered to, and we make no objections to a richly adorned centre, such as is proposed in the Terrace, where ample room is provided for all the really worthy works of art that are likely to be produced here in a hundred years; but we plead for the preservation, as far as possible, of largeness

BIRD CAGE.

and simplicity, for the greatest amount of unobstructed lawn, for trees, and shrubbery, and flowers; for lakes and streams; in short, for as much of nature as we can get for money, and for a very little art, and that only of the choicest and best.

But, lest the reader should think we have brought him up

this pretty hillock, not so much to see the statue of the Tigress as to hear a lecture, we offer him our convoy down again and across the plaza to the Casino, or Ladies' Refreshment House, where, as that intended for gentlemen is not yet built, we must

DRINKING FOUNTAIN.

content ourselves with whatever airy food is provided for the gentler sex. On our way thither we stop for a moment to watch the play of the two fountains, or of the birds in their gilded cages, or to drink from one of these elegant basins of bronze and polished granite, whose never-failing streams of iced water are in such constant demand through the long summer days. But we may all drink our fill, for the great reservoirs yonder are our inexhaustible cisterns, and beneath our feet are deep pits filled with blocks of ice, over which the water flows before it falls into these cool basins.

The fountains on the plaza are extremely pretty, and curious beside. There has been no attempt to show us large streams of water rising to a great height. Such jets would not be suitable to this situation, for one reason among others, that the area of the plaza is not very large, and, as it is often filled with people, the wind blowing the spray about, would produce a good deal of discomfort. These lighter and more graceful fountains have therefore been introduced, and they are found to be equally interesting to grown philosophers as to children. They are in fact philosophical toys, and one of them, at least, presents a problem that has never yet been satisfactorily solved. A little hollow ball of metal, perforated here and there over its whole surface with small holes, is seen to dance the whole day long upon the end of a slender perpendicular jet of water. Nothing can be more graceful than the light balancing of this ball, and much debate does the fancy trifle give rise to among bearded men who are quite above all suspicion of being amused with the toy at which the merry circle of eager children clap their hands and laugh with unrestrained delight. The other fountains are on a different principle, allied, perhaps, to that which gives motion to the familiar firework-wheels and serpents. Small jets are made of pieces of brass tubing variously curved, and radiating from a common centre with which they all communicate. One of these is set upon the end of the upright fountain pipe, and as soon as the water is let on it sets the wheel to spinning, and once in motion it continues to move until the water is drawn off. The principle once discovered is capable of a great variety of applications, and a good deal of ingenuity has been shown in the devising of new jets.

Lord Bacon, in his essay, "Of Gardens," speaks of these toy

fountains as if they were not uncommon in his time:—"And for fine Devices, of Arching Water without Spilling, and Making it rise in severall Formes (of Feathers, Drinking Glasses, Canopies, and the like) they be pretty things to looke on, but Nothing to Health and Sweetnesse." Tennyson, too, in his "Princess," published in 1848, thus sings of these toys:—

> "For all the sloping pasture murmured sown
> With happy faces and with holiday.
> There moved the multitude, a thousand heads:
> The patient leaders of their Institute
> Taught them with facts. One reared a font of stone
> And drew, from butts of water on the slope,
> The fountain of the moment, playing now
> A twisted snake, and now a rain of pearls,
> Or steep-up spout whereon the gilded ball
> Danced like a wisp."

At one end of the plaza we see a number of light iron chairs piled up, and in charge of them a man who informs us that they are to be hired for a trifling sum by any one who wishes a seat. This is the system pursued abroad, as many of our readers will remember, but the admirable police regulations of the Central Park do not permit the entrapping of unwary visitors that is practised in the London parks—in the St. James', as we know by experience, and as we heard in others. In the St. James' Park the enterprising lessee sets seats about at various points removed from his main stand, and taking good care not to affix any sign or mark by which the stranger may know that they are private property, he then retires to his stand, and assuming a nonchalant or pre-occupied air, watches with unremitting vigilance the approach of his unconscious victim. That person being a rural Englishman or a travelling American, seeing a chair agreeably planted under a shady tree, seats himself carelessly in it, and draws out of his pocket a book to beguile the hour. No sooner has he become absorbed in his reading than he is roused by the presence of an unattractive man, who, grinning maliciously, draws open his coat in an ostentatious manner and displays a large badge on which is inscribed the information that he is the owner of the chair on which the stranger is seated, and that he expects to be paid, then and there, for the use of the same. The English or Continental visitor being used to varied and perpetual payments exacted for any thing and every thing, at once complies with the demand and gets rid of the bore; but the annoyed American, disgusted with the smallness of the sixpenny-extorting device, is Quixotic enough to resist and argue. The infuriated spider, who has never before met with a remonstrating fly, coaxes, wheedles, blusters, swears, and threatens, but, being met with that serenity which always marks the demeanor of those who wage war for principle, and finding that the penny for which he had so elaborately plotted shows no intention of emerging from the seclusion of its owner's pocket, he begins a warlike dance accompanied with the snapping of his fingers by way of castanets, and, foaming with rage, proceeds to deny to that owner any right to the sacred name of gentleman. The last seen of him by the American as he quietly walks away, having given the sixpence to one of the million beggars who are always on the *qui vive* in London, and who are by no means always dressed in rags, he is dancing a series of pirouettes in front of the empty seat, that for the first time, perhaps, in his experience, has failed to catch the expected prey.

The Commissioners of the Central Park have wisely prevented the possibility of any such small but irritating annoyances as this within the limits of their jurisdiction. They would, doubtless, prefer that every thing in the Park should be freely enjoyed by the visitors; but, since the means at their disposal do not permit this in all cases, they have done all that can be done to prevent any misunderstanding as to fees, and to make them so small that hardly any one need feel himself deprived of a simple pleasure by its cost. We suppose they would be glad to exercise more control than is permitted them over the hacks that carry strangers round the Park, and this may come in time; meanwhile they prevent the rapacity of the drivers to the extent allowed them, and the stranger may be sure of hospitable treatment from every one within the gates. A small charge is made for the use of the boats on the Lake, and for the chairs— although these are an experiment, hardly adopted as yet for a permanence. Beside these and the carriages, which do not belong to the Park, there is nothing except refreshments that the visitor may not freely enjoy. No shows of any kind are allowed on the Park grounds; no jugglers, gamblers—except those disguised as gentlemen—puppet-shows, pedlers of flowers, players upon so-called musical instruments, ballad-singers, nor hand-organ men; in fact none of the great army of small persecutors who torment the outside world, can enter into this pleasant place to make us miserable in it. Nor is there to be found a guide in the whole Park. If you want to be directed, you can ask your way of a policeman, who would lose his place if he were known to take a fee. If you like to be lost you are at liberty to do so, and every year a hundred or so little children exercise that precious privilege, and are returned to their tranquil parents without loss of time, and without expense to anybody. No one who has not been in England or on the Continent can know how great a blessing it is to have got rid of that ubiquitous nuisance, a guide; to be able to go where one wills; to see, or not to see; to sit and muse, to sit and read, without having superfluous advice thrust upon one, or being obliged to receive information for which he has no natural appetite, and to hear questions answered that he has never asked.

The Casino is a pretty domestic-looking little cottage, planted upon the rising ground east of the plaza, and designed as a Ladies' House of Refreshment. There are two large rooms, one at each end, connected by a long apartment opening upon a central piazza. Here one can procure almost any kind of light refreshment, every thing provided, as in ordinary restau-

THE CASINO FROM THE EAST.

rants, being at a fixed price clearly stated in the bill of fare. The visitor will, we dare say, be pleased to find that what has been judged most likely to suit the delicate appetites of ladies is astonishingly like the sort of things the sterner sex delight in, and if he be a reasonable man, content with a very little provender for a good deal of money, he will easily be able to make a comfortable meal. Of course, the proprietor of this establishment, as well as the head of the larger and more hotel-like restaurant of Mount St. Vincent, has mainly in view the making of money, and this is quite right, but the Commissioners care only, as in duty bound, for the welfare and enjoyment of the public, and they have therefore made it a condition in

leasing these places, that they shall be at all times subject to
their examination and approval, the proprietors being, in a sort,
their agents, and bound to regulate their establishments in con-
formity with the general principles of the Park management,
beside the more particular conditions imposed in the lease.
Thus, every episode of the Park is under the control of one
authority—that of the Commissioners—and no conflict is possible between those appointed by the people to rule and regulate
the Park, and the persons who are, in effect, employed by them to
assist in carrying out particular parts of their general scheme.

VINERY NEAR CASINO, OVERLOOKING THE MALL.

The Casino is immediately surrounded by trees and shrubbery, except on one side where it looks out upon the Carriage
Concourse, as it is called, a large rectangle of gravel, approached
by a short arm leading from the main eastern drive nearly opposite Seventieth Street. Here on every music-day will be found
a circle of carriages, whose owners either sit in them listening
to the music in the Mall that runs just below the hill, or eat

creams and ices in the Casino, or enjoy the pleasant shade of
the Vinery with its cheerful outlook upon the crowd that throngs
the Mall, and roams or rests upon the broad stretches of the
close-clipt lawns. This Vinery, when the wisterias, honeysuckles, and roses that already make a light curtain over it, are
fully grown, will be one of the pleasantest resting-places in the

SUMMER HOUSE NEAR HAMILTON SQUARE.

Park. When the light western breezes that refresh our summer
twilight begin to spring up from the near-flowing river, no wonder that hither come—

> "many a pair of friends,
> Who, arm in arm, enjoy the warm
> Moon-births and the long evening-ends."

for few cities any where have such a charming promenade.

Southeast of the Casino, on a rocky knoll very near the Fifth Avenue, is one of the many pretty rustic summer-houses that tempt the visitor to stop and rest in his walk. This belongs to the class of shelters rather than to that of the summer-houses proper, for the walk passes directly through it and down the hill on the other side. A number of well-grown oaks and willows, relics of the original vegetation, grow near it; and on the ground at the foot of the knoll, and, wherever it has been possible, in the shallow earth, that covers the knoll itself in places, evergreens have been closely planted, and have already attained a considerable growth. By the time the city fairly reaches this point in its march toward Harlem, this summer-house will be so shut off from the view of passers in the street, above which, beside, it is elevated more than twenty feet, that one can find here almost as complete a seclusion, for an hour's reading or meditation, as

OAKS NEAR ARSENAL.

he could obtain in the centre of the Park itself, so judicious has been the planting, begun at the very earliest possible moment, and so promising the growth up to the present time.

Directly opposite the knoll on which this shelter is placed, on the opposite or east side of the Fifth Avenue, is Hamilton Square, an open space belonging to the city, and extending from the Fifth to the Fourth Avenue, between Sixty-sixth and Sixty-eighth streets. It contains fifteen acres, and is thus of considerable size, having six more acres than Washington Square, and five more than the Battery, the City Hall Park, or Tompkins Square. Like all the squares belonging to the city, this is under the control, not of the Central Park Commissioners, but of the Street Commissioner, and it will, therefore, be laid out probably in the same homespun way that the others have been; but every such opening in the wall of houses that must some day surround the

SUMMER-HOUSE SOUTHEAST OF THE CASINO.

Park is a welcome relief, and aids in producing something of the effect of irregularity of outline in which the Park is unfortunately wanting. Hamilton Square is the only green bay of this sort that relieves the monotonous length of the Fifth Avenue along the whole line of the Park. Artistically, and, we have no doubt, financially, this is a great mistake, and it is much to be desired that if the opening of additional squares be no longer possible—even where one is so much needed as it is between Eighty-fifth and Ninety-seventh streets, opposite the new Reservoir—owners of property in that and in other quarters would, at least, see the advantage, both to themselves and the public, of so building on their lots as to secure all the light and air possible, with the additional attraction of grass and trees. This would be very easily accomplished if the owners of the lots forming the several blocks would combine to make "Terraces" or "Crescents," as is so often done in London, particularly in the new and fashionable West-End, a sort of arrangement that adds greatly to the elegance of that part of the city, and largely increases the value of the property. Those of our readers who may not know just what we mean, will find an illustration in the familiar "London Terrace" on Twenty-third Street, between the Ninth and Tenth avenues, and also in the arrangement of the lots on the Fourth Avenue, between Seventeenth and Eighteenth streets. The terraces in London are not exactly like these, and indeed they are by no means laid out on any one model, but they almost all, we believe, have a private carriage-road and sidewalk running along close to the house-fronts, while the garden space, with its grass, and trees, and flowers, is between this private roadway and the public street. In the crescents— of which, so far as we know, there is no example in any of our Atlantic cities—this private road is an arc of a circle, to which the house-fronts correspond. The principle is the same in both, but perhaps in the minds of our New-Yorkers there might be an objection to this partial seclusion which is the very thing sought for in the London plan of terrace and crescent. In case this objection should be felt, there need be no private drive, but the house might be reached by the walk from the gate on the public street through the garden, as in the already familiar New York examples.

But it ought, we think, to be evident that some such device as this must be adopted if it is hoped to maintain the traditional elegance of the Fifth Avenue. In any case, the street is too uninterrupted in its length, and greatly lacks incident. As was very well shown recently by Mr. Leopold Eidlitz, one of our most accomplished architects, there is no example of a fine street anywhere in Europe that is also a very long street:— 'In Paris a boulevard or a street is rarely carried to a length greater than two thousand feet, without being interrupted by a square, or changing its direction, or terminating upon a park, or opening upon something other than itself." This applies directly and forcibly to the Fifth Avenue as well as to Broadway, which Mr. Eidlitz had more immediately in his mind when he wrote. Between Washington Square, where it begins, and the Central Park, the only break in the monotony of the Fifth Avenue occurs at Madison Square, where, beside, the intersection of the avenue with Broadway gives us the small triangular lot on which is placed the Worth Monument. From this point again the avenue stretches to the Park, lined with a double row of houses, more remarkable for the evidence they give of the diffusion of wealth in the community than for their architectural merit. It is now more than probable that the lower half of the avenue—between Washington Square and Twenty-third Street— will be given up to shops and stores, and that the efforts in architecture of the next generation will be made in the upper portion nearer to the Park and along its eastern line. The new Jewish synagogue, the new Romish cathedral, with some of the latest private houses, that of Mr. Martin, for instance, all point in this direction. But it is altogether likely that the wealth of the future will make its most splendid displays in the immediate vicinity of the Park, on the two avenues that bound it to the east and west, and it is therefore of the greatest importance, as regards the beauty of this vicinity, that some theory of building should be adopted at the outset that will prevent the reproach of monotony being brought against our city in the future as it has been in the past. It is now too late, doubtless, to break up the formal arrangement of the streets in that part of the city that lies below One-Hundred-and-Tenth Street, but a great deal may yet be done to make that formality less offensively apparent. It does not concern us here to show how this can be accomplished in other parts of the city, nor to prove to owners of property that their real-estate would lose nothing in value by being less closely built upon; but it belongs strictly to our subject to remonstrate against the surrounding the Park itself with a close line of houses, however elegant and costly, even if every house were such a finished jewel-box as that recently built by Mr. Mould for Mr. Martin. Such a wall of brick and stone, broken at regular intervals by streets, would be in the highest degree ineffective, and the drive along it would be wearisome and uninteresting, if for no other reason, because of the want of balance between the two sides, all trees on the one, all masonry on the other. The arrangement that ought to be adopted at the outset, as it seems to us, is either that which we have already proposed of terraces and crescents, or else a mixture of these with small open squares of the width of a single block, surrounded with low copings of stone, planted with grass and trees, and open at all times to the people, or, if they are private property, then reserved like Gramercy, Stuyvesant, and the late St. John's, squares, for the use of the occupants of the surrounding houses. Devices like these, simple in execution, and paying for themselves by the greatly increased value they would give to the property in their neighborhood, would effectually lighten up the sides of the avenues opposite the Park, and prevent the monotony that is at present threatened.

We suggest too, that such open squares as those we propose

would be the most appropriate places for the erection of the museums of History, Art, Science, and Natural History that we may not unreasonably hope will one day redeem New York from the charge of being the worst provided city in this respect in the world in proportion to her size, and, we may add, in proportion to her municipal pretensions. Until she have them she can never be a great city in any true sense of the term. Wanting these, she may be an overgrown Hamburg or Frankfort, but she can never be a London or a Paris. And, small as is the progress that has been made at the present time in supplying the need of these things, there can be no doubt that we shall have them in time, or that, when they come, they will be worthy of the city. It is too early to look for the establishment of institutions of this kind, which spring up naturally only when certain material conditions of growth and wealth have been fulfilled, and the culture that is the fruit of these has made considerable progress. But it will not do to wait too long before planting at least the seeds of these institutions in places favorable to their growth. The Astor Library, the Historical Society, the Academy of Design, the Society of Natural History, ought all to secure land near the Park, and to hold it for a term of years, even if this can be done in no other way than by putting up temporary dwelling-houses, and leasing them until they themselves are in a condition to erect buildings suitable for their collections. Then if the idea of squares, similar to Hamilton Square, opening upon the Park, here and there along its side, can be carried out, what admirable situations will thus be provided for the future institutions of literature, art, and science. For such societies do not need to have their homes on crowded and fashionable streets, but are best placed when, without being out of the way, or difficult of access, they are removed from noise and bustle, and the distraction of the outside world, and, beside, can receive abundant supplies of light and air from every side.

WESTERN HALF OF TERRACE, FROM THE MUSIC-STAND.

We have already called attention to the fact that the carriage drive, which crosses the Terrace, forms a nearly direct communication between the Fifth and the Eighth avenues at Seventy-second Street. These are the first points north of Fifty-ninth Street on either avenue where the Park can be entered. On the Eighth Avenue opposite Seventy-second Street is the Women's Gate, and on the Fifth Avenue opposite the same street is the Children's Gate. Entering then, at either of these gates, the visitor will find himself, after a short walk, or a few turns of the wheels, at a point where he strikes the main road running north and south, while the road by which he entered keeps due east or west. We have now reached this point, descending from the Casino, and as we have already seen

SKATING WEST OF BOW BRIDGE.

the Terrace, and neither wish to leave the Park at Seventy-second Street, nor to retrace our steps to the south, we will continue our drive toward the north, and seek the rural beauty of the Ramble.

The road at first strikes inland, and shortly skirts the eastern end of the Lake. On our right the ground sinks sensibly in a shallow hollow, the bottom of which is some twelve feet below the level of the Lake itself. Here is a pretty piece of ornamental water, consisting of a large symmetrical basin with a border of cut stone, and with a fountain in the centre. This basin is filled by the overflow of the Lake, and by whatever additional water is supplied from the drainage of the hollow in which it lies. This hollow, as will easily be seen by reference to the plan, is a continuation of the second of the two depressions which mark the lower half of the Park, and of which we have already spoken. Originally this was all a marsh, extending completely across the entire tract of the Park land; and in Mr. Viele's design the drainage was collected into three small and insignificant pools connected by a running stream, two of them being on the site of the present Lake, and the other between this ornamental water and the road leading from Seventy-second Street. No one can fail to see that much more has been gained for the Park, both in beauty and utility, by the treatment of Messrs. Vaux and Olmsted. The drive at the east end of the Lake—where the reader is supposed to be at present—passes from one side of this hollow to the other, over a solid bridge of stone with a railing of gilded iron, and pierced with a trefoil-shaped archway for the accommodation of a foot-path leading to the ornamental water with its surrounding flower-beds. Thus the drive, at this point looks down upon two very different views. On the one side is the Lake, with the pretty verdure of the Ramble on its north shore, the lower plaza of the Terrace on its south, the Bow Bridge far to the west, and its shining surface glinting with the flash of oars, or traced with silver furrows by the slow-gliding swans; or, in the winter, gay with the merry groups of skaters who stream from one division of the pond to the other under the graceful arch of the Bow Bridge.   On the other side we see the meadow-hollow, dotted with trees and flowering shrubs, and in the midst the ornamental water with its formal architectural border, in direct contrast to the irregular Lake with its rocky and wooded juttings in and out, and this formality further emphasized by the par-

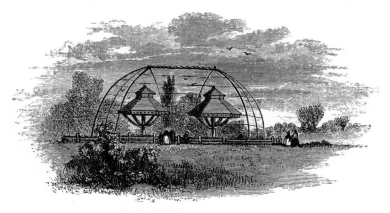

THE DOVECOTE.

terre, with its set walks, and flowers in masses of color enclosed in geometric figures.   On the extreme eastern edge of this garden-hollow it was once intended to place a conservatory of two stories height, to be entered from the Park and from the Fifth Avenue, and the contract for building it was actually taken by Messrs. Parsons & Co., of Flushing, Long Island. But, just then, the war broke out, and this enterprise, with many others, was brought to a stand, and has never since been revived. This is much to be regretted, for the plan was an excellent one, and the character of the gentlemen who proposed to take charge of it was such as to be an ample guaranty that the undertaking would be in all respects well managed.   The plan of the building was double, embracing two stories, and the elevation showed the heights of these stories in its double curve of glass, the lower one projecting far beyond the upper, and the upper one topped by a ventilating clear-story also of glass. The lower floor, entered from a central door on the eastern side of the ornamental water, and also by an ample stair-way from the upper division, contained two large rooms, one at either end—the Fernery and the Camellia Room, each having its own external door. On either hand, as the visitor entered the hall from below, and facing west, were the Flower Rooms, where cut flowers and bouquets were to be kept for sale. On the opposite side, nearly against the wall of the Park, were the furnaces and offices, and thus the centre of the hall, with its light pillars supporting the floor above, was left free for the movement of visitors. Up-stairs was the conservatory, fully lighted on all sides, and on a level with the Fifth Avenue, from which it could be entered, as well as from below. It was intended to make this conservatory useful as well as beautiful by adopting a more natural arrangement than can easily be contrived in smaller buildings. It was designed to give each plant, so far as possible, an opportunity to grow in its own way, and to develop all its propensities without the restraint of the etiquette usually enforced in these places. Thus, while all the ordinary effects of growth and bloom would be obtained here in full measure, we should have had, beside, the added pleasure of seeing how these pretty prisoners grow when free; how they spread, and climb or creep; and thus making a sort of useful acquaintance with them. As the plans of the Commissioners were so fully developed with regard to this conservatory, and as Mr. Vaux's design was so carefully studied, and so well conceived, we will hope the idea is not wholly abandoned, and that before a great while we may see the sparkle of these glass roofs answering the far-off sparkle of the Lake.

To the north of the ornamental water, and in the tract between the main drive and the Fifth Avenue, there are several points of minor interest, although this part of the Park is but little frequented yet, owing, perhaps to its immediate vicinity to the Ramble. The tract is divided into two distinct parts by a branch of the main carriage-drive, leading in a diagonal to the Miners' Gate, at Seventy-ninth Street; and the bridle-path also

OAKS NEAR SEVENTY-NINTH STREET ENTRANCE.

crosses it in a direction nearly north and south. This bridle-path runs on each side of an irregular oval where grow some picturesque young oaks that have already attained a consider-able size, and whose shade is very welcome in the heat of summer, as we know by experience, having passed many an hour under them with our book. Just beyond these oaks, as will be seen by the cut, the bridle-path passes under the branch carriage-road above mentioned, by an arch in a substantial viaduct of light-colored stone, with a railing composed of stone balusters and piers. Looking up from our book or newspaper, we see across the lawn, the Dovecotes under their high-arched prison of wire, of which we have already given an illustration. And still further

on we shall find the pretty " Evergreen Walk," first laid out in
1862, and promising before long to become a delightful place
of resort on sunny days in winter. It consists of an encircling
wall of trained and trimmed evergreens, the general outline of
which is an elongated quatre-foil. On the outside of this wall
evergreens are planted as thickly as they will grow healthily,
and retain their natural form, and these are to be allowed to
reach their natural height. Through the centre of this enclosed
space there runs a double row of evergreens, clipped and trimmed
like the outside wall, and presenting on all four sides a smooth
wall of verdure, with cosy projecting and retreating ins and outs,
each bay provided with a seat, so that six seats on the inside
face the central walk, and six on the outside face the walk that

MOWING LAWN NEAR SEVENTY-NINTH STREET.

runs round the whole. Such an evergreen shelter needs, at least,
ten years of growth and care before it will appear all that its
designers meant to make it; but this one bids fair to be com-

pletely successful under the hands of the excellent gardener who has already performed such wonders here with his obedient trees and flowers.

The large triangular plot bounded by the main drive, the second traffic-road, and the branch carriage-road to Seventy-ninth Street, is unbroken save by the bridle-path which, passing under the branch carriage-road, ascends and crosses the traffic-road by a concealed bridge, and then, sharply turning to the left, makes for the Reservoir. The triangular plot we have just left is lightly set with trees, which crowd together into a close boscage along the traffic-road, leaving the greater part of the slope in lawn, over which we hear the rattle of the lawn-mowers' wheels that here, as on every well-regulated estate, have taken the place of the scythe with its cheerful whistle. In their report for 1866, the Commissioners say:—"The appearance of those portions of the lawn cut by the lawn-mowers is remarkably superior to that of those cut by the scythe. The sod is firmer, and the grass much more dense and even, and seems to maintain its freshness for a longer period."

On the west side of the main drive we find a turnout, directly opposite this lawn, by which we enter, and, alighting upon a broad carriage-step of cut stone, find ourselves in the Ramble at its northeast angle. This pleasant spot, to many the greatest attraction the Park contains, lies upon the southern slope of the rocky ledge that occupies the middle of the Park, sloping gradually toward the east. The Ramble is shut in between the two main drives on the east and west, and between the Lake and the old Reservoir on the south and north. It is estimated to contain about thirty-six acres, and, although it has several open spaces of lawn, it is, for the most part, quite thickly planted with trees and shrubbery, and laid out with a multitude of

TERRACE FROM ROCK IN RAMBLE.

irregular and interlacing walks, arranged without any definite
plan. It would have been difficult for one who surveyed this
site before the Commissioners took it in hand, to believe that ten
years could so thoroughly transform it. It was then, as we well
remember, an unsightly mass of particularly barren rock, on
which even mosses and lichens refused to grow; the soil thinly
spread between the ledges was too poor to support any but the
toughest and least graceful shrubs, while along its centre there
ran a bit of soggy marsh that held the drainage of the higher
portion until it could leak down into the still lower valley, or
until it should be dried up under the heat of the August suns.
To-day no rock is seen but such as is needed for picturesque
variety; the rest is covered with earth, or overlaid so thick with
honeysuckle, wild grape, trumpet-creeper, or wisteria, that its
presence is not suspected by the passer-by. From April to
September the Ramble is filled with the delightful perfume
of these honeysuckles, while to these is added, in June, July,
and August, the even more delicate odor of the swamp magnolia (*M. glauca*). Bacon, in that pretty passage in his Essay
of Gardens, beginning, "And because the Breath of Flowers
is farre Sweeter in the Aire (where it comes and goes like
the Warbling of Musick) than in the Hand, therefore nothing
is more fit for that Delight than to know, what be the
Flowers, and Plants, that doe best perfume the Aire,"—after
giving a long list, whose names, with his quaint comments,
read like a nosegay, brings in the honeysuckle:—"Then, the
Hony Suckles," he says, "so they be somewhat a farre off."
Here we may have them as we will, "farre" or "neare," and
of the different kinds of honeysuckle (*Lonicera*) the Park
gardener can show us seventeen—nineteen—if we count two
that are rather shrubs than climbers. However, most of these
are odorless. As for the magnolia, it used to be a rare plant
in our northern soil, growing, we believe, only in two places,

and those far apart: the Jersey swamps, and in one particular spot in Gloucester, Massachusetts, where flourishes a
small and isolated clump of this tree with its delightfully aro-
matic flowers, a waif of the tropics, seemingly cast ashore on
these stormy rocks. Of late years it has been more frequently
found in gardens, and the numerous specimens contained in the
Park will, ere long, make it still more familiar.

The design in planting the Ramble has been to give, if possible, the delicate flavor of wildness, so hard to seize and imprison
when civilization has once put it to flight. Therefore, an effort
has been made to bring into these bounds as many of the wood
flowers and flowering shrubs, the native growths of our forests,
as would thrive here—foreign flowers and imported shrubs being
put in places more seeming artificial. The success has been
considerable, and every year adds something to the list, so
that already the city boy or girl may find here the earliest
anemones, hepaticas, blood-roots, adders'-tongues, columbines, and
last, not least, the blessed dandelions, in such beautiful profusion as we have never seen elsewhere, making the lawns, in
places, like green lakes reflecting a heaven sown with stars.
And in time we have no doubt that the Ramble will become
a favorite resort for teachers of botany with their broods of
learners, since the city suburbs are getting to be so thickly
built up that it is not easy to find a haunt where the wild
flowers can grow undisturbed, while here they will always be
found in profusion, and though the laws of the Park forbid
that they should be pulled, yet their habits of growth may be
studied, and the young be made familiar with their pretty faces.
One beautiful wild flower we, ourselves, especially miss: the
Fringed Gentian (*Gentiana crinita*), celebrated by Bryant in one
of his best-known poems, and not to be spared in any collection
of our rustic beauties. It would be by no means difficult to
domesticate in a place like the Ramble, where its native habi-

tat could be almost exactly matched, and we hope, before long, to see—

> "its sweet and quiet eye
> Look through its fringes to the sky.
> Blue—blue—as if that sky let fall
> A flower from its cerulean wall."

About the middle of the Ramble a spring rises that feeds a slender stream which runs a short course till it falls into the Lake in its eastern division. This stream really drains what

NOOK IN RAMBLE.

used to be a depression across the western half of the hillside on which the Ramble lies. It is no longer a marsh, but in one or two spots the ground is purposely left but partially drained in order that certain wild plants—reeds, lilies, irises, cardinal-flowers, and others that love such watery places, may have a home, and, not less, certain birds—storks, cranes, ducks, of the choicer and rarer sorts, pelicans, and herons. In at least three places this slender thread of water is allowed to spread into shallow ponds, where, besides the flowers we have named, the visitor may find the water-lily, a shy guest, which has, however, under gentle hands, consented to bloom in these quiet and home-like waters.

RUSTIC BRIDGE IN RAMBLE.

Near the western boundary of the Ramble the brook falls over the slope that rises abruptly from a narrow creek in the

Lake—a cleft in fact in the rock—in a very pretty cascade, which makes a cheerful music in this quiet spot; while, just below, it is crossed by this Rustic Bridge, leaning over whose side we look up the stream, where, on the slip of sandy beach, we see the birds preening their feathers for another plunge, or, turning, we look on the other hand upon the shining levels of the Lake.

Further up the stream is still another Rustic Bridge in a more secluded spot, where the runnel spreads into a reedy pool, where the two pretty wood-ducks, which used to have their haunt here-

FALL IN RAMBLE.

abouts, but which are long since dead, we believe, were often to be found, in company with the distinguished-looking grey cranes, which have also yielded to fate, and whose places have not yet been supplied. We miss the stately creatures with their meditative ways, and wish them back again. A good deal of their apparent wisdom was, we suspect, imaginary. We doubt if all their profound cogitations had any other object than to decide what would be the best place to put their other foot down upon, in case they should conclude to put it down at all.

Mr. Horace Greeley is said to have remarked when he went over the Park for the first time, "Well, they have let it alone a good deal more than I thought they would!" and while there was truth in the remark it yet showed a certain misapprehension which our shrewd townsman shares in common with a great many intelligent people. But, in general, much labor must be expended before any piece of ground in a natural state can be made into a park suitable for a great city. Nor are people agreed as to

RUSTIC BRIDGE.

what the character of such a park should be. Many think that with good roads and walks, broad lawns and well-grown trees, all that is necessary, and all that is desirable will have been provided. Others would prefer something much more arti-ficial, more regular walks, a crowd of statues, water-works like those at Versailles, in short another Versailles if possible, and as much drearier and grander as money could make it. We had a fearful warning of what these people would make of a public park, in the gateways that were designed for ours a few years ago, and which we so narrowly escaped seeing erected. And still a third party are for a union of nature and art, with as much nature and as little art as can be contrived: and this would seem to have been the aim of our Central Park Commissioners. We dare say, if they had had put into their hands a broad and beautiful piece of ground, pleasantly undulating, with enough of rising hill and answering hollow, and broad reaches of lawn-like meadow, with perhaps a winding stream, that they would have felt it best to look well to the drainage, secure walks and roads as near perfection as modern skill can make, plant trees wherever nature had meant to set them, but had forgotten, and then to hold their hands.

RUSTIC SUMMER-HOUSE IN RAMBLE.

But people are mistaken who think there are, anywhere, many such places as this in the world, for there are not many acres in any one spot that would not need more skill and engineering to produce the result the "lovers of nature" delight in, than they think necessary. And, beside, it is to be remembered that, even if we had once secured such a spot, its daily use by the swarming multitudes of a great city would render it impossible to keep its rural beauty long unspoiled. The grass can never be used freely for games, for lounging, for romping, and for walking, without being destroyed, as is plainly seen in the London parks, which, in spite of their size, present in midsummer a very shabby appearance. The beautiful "common" in our neighbor city of Boston affords an illustration nearer home. The lower part has long been used by boys for playing ball and other games, and by the militia for drill. It has been found utterly impossible to keep the grass growing under such conditions, and the attempt has been abandoned. The consequence is, that this part of the common is at present a dreary waste of sand, most unsightly to look upon, and the citizens are beginning to discuss the advisability of taking away the ancient prerogatives of the boys and the soldiery. People who will consider the expense of keeping the Central Park roads in condition even when such care is taken that they be not misused, can understand what this expense would be if the restrictions were removed altogether; and those who have enjoyed the comfort of walking in our Park undisturbed by the presence of carriages or horseback-riders on the same paths, will admit that their pleasure would be seriously interfered with if they had to share the common road with vehicles and horsemen, or to take, for refuge, to an impromptu foot-path through the damp or dusty grass.

For our part we are convinced that even if a purely rural park could be made, and kept up (this last a condition almost impossible to fulfil), in the heart of a great city, it would not meet, we will not say the tastes, but the absolute requirements of the majority. In the case of our Park it must be remembered that for the site on which it was decided to plant it, nature had hardly expended the slightest effort. We might quote here the description given of it in the earlier reports by the architect-in-chief, but it is unnecessary. Many of our readers can well remember the squalor and barrenness of the un-

NOOK IN RAMBLE.

sightly spot. And those who did not see it before it was re-deemed, can at any time know what it was like to nose, and eye, and ear, by visiting some of those portions of our city, along its upper eastern and western shores, where the shanties and piggeries of the Irish crown the rocky heights, and the market-gardens and cabbage-plots fill the lower ground. A more unpromising locality was never given to any Adam to make an Eden of, and few persons who have not watched the progress of the Park from its commencement, can fully understand that its present condition is almost entirely an artificial product. Nature having done almost nothing, art had to do all. And yet art, trying to contradict nature in nothing, but only to follow her hints, improve her slight suggestions, and take advantage of her help, however stingily it may sometimes seem to have been proffered, has been able to produce a result, which, on

the whole, so closely resembles nature, that it is no wonder if the superficial observer does not clearly see how vast is the amount of work that had to be performed before the Park could reach its present perfection.

Nowhere in the Park, as it seems to us, has the result achieved been more worthy of the money, labor, and thought expended to produce it, than in the Ramble. Here at least we may be thankful that the Commissioners have not been content with merely "letting alone." For the Ramble is, in almost every

ENTRANCE TO CAVE.

square foot of it, a purely artificial piece of landscape gardening. Yet the art of concealing art was hardly ever better illustrated.

And every year's growth of trees and shrubbery makes the nature more, and the art less, so that, in time, it will only be the nature that will attract attention, and the art will be lost sight of. Already it is a delightfully retired place to which to bring one's favorite book, or to come to in the summer heats that make our city houses so unendurable, and do our thinking under the shadow of green leaves. Here a man may sit for hours and hear no sound but the chirp and twitter of the birds, the rustle of the light breeze overhead, or the far-off murmur of the town. Sometimes a nurse with her charge passes, sauntering by, sometimes a band of children, or a solitary like ourselves; but we are far from the crowd

CAVE FROM LAKE.

which, except on music-days and Sundays, does not find in the Ramble's peace and still seclusion, the excitement it comes to the Park to seek.

On the extreme western border of the Ramble will be found the Cave, a great attraction to boys and girls, and hardly less to many children of a larger growth. A steep path skirting a bank thickly set with rhododendrons, laurels, and azaleas, which make a splendid display of color in the time of bloom, leads to the foot of a large mass of rock, where a sharp turn to the left brings us to the Cave. At first, the entrance is very dark, and causes many a palpitation in tender breasts, but a few steps bring

INTERIOR OF CAVE.

us to the light, and in a moment we find ourselves looking out upon a peaceful cove, an arm of the Lake, as will be seen by the plan, where the ducks perhaps are at play, or the swans, with their young, are preening their snow-white feathers with their black bills, on the shore. Keeping close to the rocks at the right, we come to the foot of a rough stair-way of rude stone, and climbing up we reach the summit of the great rock out of which the cave is hewn. From this point we get a very pretty

ARM OF LAKE FROM CAVE.

view of the Lake at its western end, and passers-by in the boats can also look up the narrow cove at our feet, and catch a glimpse of the mouth of the Cave.

If, instead of turning into the Cave on reaching the foot of the rock, we had kept straight on, we should have come to the stone arch by which one of the many foot-paths hereabouts leads up to the same summit we gained by climbing from the Cave. This arch is built up of rough blocks of stone, and is already well covered with the vines that in no long time it is hoped will hide its masonry entirely from view. The path that leads to it, and that runs under it around the rock, is only partly arti- ficial, for if the visitor examines closely he will see that it has

RUSTIC STONE ARCH IN RAMBLE.

been formed by merely filling up the bottom of a cleft between two strata of the gneiss rock, which forms so large a part of the substratum of the Park, and whose natural dip is such that in many cases, as here, for example, it only needs slight help from the hand of man, to lend itself to the most picturesque effects. The arch in reality is a means of getting from the top of one ledge to the top of another; and the path under it is merely a cleft between the two ledges that was once filled up with some softer rock, now washed away, or which has been crumbled into sand. The summit of the stone arch can be reached either by a foot-path from the north that leads directly over it, or, on climbing out of the Cave, by keeping on the path that leads to the right.

From the top of the arch a pretty view of the Lake at its enclosed western end may be had; and on leaving it one can either descend into the Cave, or, by keeping past the rocky stair-way, make his

RUSTIC STONE ARCH IN RAMBLE—ANOTHER VIEW.

way, by a path thick set with evergreens, into the Ramble again.

As will be seen by the plan, this western side of the Ramble, compared with the eastern, is the more irregular. It contains much the greater quantity of apparent rock, and as it would be almost impossible to cover these exposed slopes and ledges with earth, the Commissioners have, in many cases, not attempted it, but have contented themselves with filling in wherever nature gave an opportunity, and covering the naked rocks with vines. Returning from the Cave, therefore, the visitor must not be surprised to find his path leading by rocky steps and steep-up ascents to the north, until at length he finds himself on a bare summit that overlooks the lower Reservoir, and sees the whole lower park lying unrolled like a map at his feet. This point of rock is, we believe, the highest in the Park, being one hundred and thirty-five feet above tide-water. An elevation in the upper park, "Great Hill," as it is

LAKE FROM TOP OF STONE ARCH.

called, near One Hundred and Fifth Street, is as high within five feet, but it does not play so important a part in the land-scape of the Park as the one on which we are at present standing. A structure called the Belvedere is in process of erection here, which is intended not merely to make a pictur-esque object seen from many points in the lower park, but to serve a useful purpose as well, being a spacious post for rest and observation. For a long time this rock has been a source of anxiety to the Commissioners, a sort of elephant on their hands that they did not know very well how to dispose of. If the reader will glance at the plan he will see that the rock is something crescent-shaped, and that it cuts into one angle of the Reservoir, preventing it from making a perfect square.   To

THE BELVEDERE.

so much of the elephant in question, the Croton Board laid

claim, and as they very naturally feared what might happen to their Reservoir in case this angle of it were tampered with, they for a long time hesitated about the expediency of giving up their title to it. Long after the southern half of the Park had reached a certain perfection, this rocky summit continued to be an eye-sore, and by no means the satisfactory terminus to the walks of this portion that, it was felt, it ought to be. But, at length, the Croton Board has been prevailed upon to allow the Park Commissioners the use of the whole of the rocky summit, and the foundations are already laid for the structure that is to be built upon it. Coming directly against the sky, as this Belvedere will, its effect as a picturesque accessory has been carefully studied, and though, in a critical mood, we might reproach it with a certain toy-like imitation of a feudal castle, perhaps this would be hardly fair. For, without doubt, the structure is really needed at this particular point, and, for the use it is to serve, it happens that the form that has been given it, is every way well adapted. A view of the proposed building was given in the tenth annual report of the Commissioners, and large drawings of the structure in perspective were placed by Messrs. Vaux and Olmsted in the last exhibition of the National Academy, so that the public is already somewhat familiar with its appearance as it will be when completed. The design includes a sort of platform, with buildings for shelter and outlook at either end. Those to the west are lower, and of a more domestic form, while at the east, a larger building of two stories with a flat roof has, at its southeastern angle, a tower of considerable height, commanding the same view that was formerly obtained from the old bell-tower: the one whose red ball used to be so anxiously looked for by thousands during the skating season. On the two gonfalons at the Terrace, the reader may remember that the arms of the State and City of New York were severally emblazoned; so, on this tower of the Belvedere, the flag of the United States will be kept flying all the year round.

VIEW FROM BELVEDERE, LOOKING SOUTH.

Under that portion of the rock that lies just south of the Belvedere is the Tunnel, constructed at great expense, for carrying the second of the traffic-roads—the one that comes out, on both avenues, at Seventy-ninth Street. This Tunnel was completed in January, 1861, and, after a careful examination, the roof was found to be sound and firm. The length of the Tunnel is one hundred and forty-six feet, and the height of the roof above the centre of the roadway, seventeen feet ten inches. Its width—forty feet—is the same as that of the road it spans, all the traffic-roads having the same dimensions. After passing through the Tunnel, the road continues in a straight line for six hundred feet parallel with the southern wall of the old Reservoir. It then takes a strong curve to the north, and comes out at Seventy-ninth Street, by the Miners' Gate. At this gate a branch of the main carriage-drive on the east side of the Park, and a branch from the bridle-path also, leave the grounds.

VIEW FROM BELVEDERE, LOOKING SOUTHEAST.

As the Ramble has no central avenue or walk, and no central point of interest, indeed, unless it be the Belvedere and the view from its tower, it is not easy to describe it, if it were necessary or desirable to do so, after any methodical plan. It is a place to ramble about in, not to walk through—a place to sit and rest in, to chat with a friend, or to read such books as one can read in the open air, where nature does not wish us to read, but to enjoy her varied and incessant play. For the matter of rest, all sorts of seats, shelters, arbors, summer-houses, abound in this beautiful retreat. A sudden turn in the path brings us to the pretty bower of which Mr. Bellows has given us a cut on page 112, where seats on either side enable the aged to rest a bit after what, to some, may be a fatiguing climb, or give excuse to a pair of lovers to pause awhile in their pleasant stroll, and debate

whether they shall continue their walk, or sit for the rest of
the day under this canopy of vine,

> —"sheltered from day's garish eye,
> While the bee with honeyed thigh,
> That at her flowery work doth sing,
> And the waters murmuring."—

if they do not entice the dewy-feathered sleep of Milton, at least
make possible many an hour of quiet enjoyment and rest in the

SUMMER-HOUSE IN RAMBLE NEAR THE BELVEDERE.

midst of the noisy city. On the summits of many of the lesser
eminences in the Ramble, shelters like this have been erected,
some of them with seats both within and without, others with
only a central pillar surrounded by a circular bench, and supporting a broad umbrella-like covering. From these seats an unin-

terrupted view may be obtained on all sides, no posts nor lattice-work shutting off the landscape; but, while several of them are constructed on this principle, no one of them is an exact copy of any other. Not only is a pleasant variety secured in this way, but visitors, whose bump of locality is small, are more easily able to fix their whereabouts, and to find their way about than they would be if they came, every now and then, upon a summer-house or seat exactly like the one they had rested on a half-hour earlier in their walk. Yet in all this variety there is nothing merely curious or fantastic: use and beauty are in every case delightfully combined, and there are few seats in the Park, we should think, upon which the oldest and feeblest person, or the most delicate convalescent would not find it easy to get the rest which, when it can be had at the needed moment, will often make a much longer walk possible than would be in the real country, almost anywhere. Sometimes these rests are not sheltered at all except by the trees and shrubs about them; or they are placed against the broad, steep side of some mossy and lichened rock; or by the border of a brook or pool, where, while we sit, the birds will alight to drink or bathe, or perhaps the brown rabbit will come hopping by, his long ears all alert with suspicious fear, and his startled eyes quick to catch sight of the intruder upon his preserve, but, with a confidence in the power of the Commissioners to protect him that is beautiful to see, soon making up his mind to eat his dinner in defiance of strangers. Others, again, are large and ample structures, capable of giving sufficient shelter to scores of people flying distractedly from the sudden shower. The summer-house near the Artists' Gate is one of the very earliest erected in the Park. Those first built were designed by a certain Hungarian, who showed a great aptitude for this kind of archi-tecture at least, and who was ably seconded by the workmen the Commissioners employed to assist him. Hardly any thing of the sort had ever been seen before in this country, but since that day a great many, almost as good in design, have been put up in various parts of the Park by other hands.   The material employed is the common cedar, which so abounds in

SUMMER-HOUSE NEAR ARTISTS' GATE.

the vicinity of New York.   The limbs and trunks are stripped of their bark, and they are then put together in a solid and workmanlike fashion, very unlike the frail and flimsy structures which we commonly meet with under the name of summer-houses.   Nor is it merely the workmanship that makes them noticeable, the design is always artistic and agreeable, and they are no less an ornament to the Park than useful and convenient buildings, without which the place would lose one of its chief attractions.   Nearly all of them are now covered with vines which, in many cases, almost conceal the frame-work, giving us, instead of artificial decoration, a profuse tracery of the most graceful vines.   Over some, the Chinese honeysuckle spreads a fragrant shade; over others the wisteria, with its parti-colored

leaves of tenderest brown and green, and its delicate purple
flowers; or the rampant trumpet-creeper, that with the larger,
and that with the smaller and finer flowers; or the wild grape
with its spring-scent sweeter than mignonette; or the pretty
gourds with their pendent bottles of yellow, green, and orange,
the delight of children. The Park gardener has a mission to
teach us all what beautiful things can be done with the simplest
means, and gets some of his most charming effects with plants

RAMBLE.

that rich men, and poor men too for that matter, sometimes
think too humble for their gardens. We remember one spot
where the whole face of a steep rock is covered with a waving

curtain of money-wort (*Lysimachia nummularia*), a pretty, little, vulgar plant, long since exiled from all aristocratic gardens, but which seems to delight in showing how, in this stately garden of the people, it can hold its own by the side of many plants with far finer names and a much prouder lineage. Some of our readers may remember having seen the money-wort growing in old-fashioned gardens in pots and boxes, sometimes standing by the borders of the walks, sometimes planted on the gate-posts, the long trailing stems regularly set with their roundish, opposite leaves and flowers. But we never before saw it growing as freely and in such masses as in the spot we speak of in the Park; it seems to have found its *habitat* here, a place exactly suited to its needs, where it may show the world all its capabilities.

Then, in another part of the Park, the soil in the long clefts of a mass of the gneiss rock is filled with the native cactus, commonly called the prickly-pear, which grows so thickly over the rocks and cliffs in New Jersey, along the Hudson River shore. It has thick, fleshy leaves, a blunt oval in shape, set all over with small bunches of very fine sharp thorns, so easily detached that it is impossible to touch the leaf without getting some of them into the flesh. The flowers, which, in the season, are very numerous, are extremely delicate and pretty, being of a bright canary yellow, and having a sort of outlandish tropical appearance that increases the pleasure of coming upon them in one's walk. Whether they were found growing wild on these rocks when the Park was first taken in hand, we do not know, but here they are to-day, mingling their large, gauze-like, yellow stars with the profuse bloom of the portulacca, and, no doubt, deceiving many with the belief that they are some rare species of cactus from foreign parts, set out here to bloom for a summer and to be tenderly nursed and housed during the coming winter.

In the same way, the Park gardener has introduced many of

our native plants hitherto despised, or little known, and by securing for them conditions favorable to their growth has enabled us to
become familiar with some that we should otherwise have long
continued strangers to. We have already spoken of the swamp-
magnolia. Before the Park was planted it was rare in our Northern States, and confined as it was to two spots, and those of
small extent, there was a probability that before long it might
disappear from our soil altogether. But specimens were early
planted in the Ramble, and have thriven so well, and are in
such profusion, that the Jersey swamps and Massachusetts Gloucester can no longer claim a monopoly of this delightful shrub.
We regard it as one of the chief advantages of the Park, one
of the ways in which it can most usefully serve the public, this
fostering of our native plants, setting them before the public in
such a way as to make us all acquainted with their good points
and with their beauties, which, but for this introduction, we
might have long remained ignorant of. This is in some respects, for practical purposes, the best sort of botanical garden.
Of course it is not the sort that a scientific man will desire, but
it probably teaches the general public more than a more formal
scientific arrangement would, perhaps for the very reason that
it makes no pretence of teaching us at all. We make the acquaintance of many trees, shrubs, vines, and flowers here in a
familiar, easy way, as we would of people in their homes. They
are not on their dignity here, they grow as they like best, and
the gardener is one of those rare members of his class who
knows enough to let his subjects have their own way, or think
they are having it. Who ever knew, unless he had travelled
in England, where gardening is understood as nowhere else in
the world, what the honeysuckle can do when it can follow its
own inclination, and is not urged to climb a trellis it has no
mind for? What a sight for the eye, what a feast to the nose,
this great rock covered with a cataract of bloom, the tendril-spray

tossed into the air as it pours down upon the grass, and the bees
about it in a humming cloud.   Here is another rocky slope covered with the trumpet-creeper, the long branches loving the
warmth creep down among the grass, and the flowers peeping
up surprise us with unknown blooms among the homespun
dandelions and clover-heads.   In a large estate like the Central
Park, the gardener can often give us the opportunity of studying the effects produced by plants growing in large masses, and
in a soil, and under conditions, exactly suited to their needs,
an opportunity which we can seldom enjoy in any private garden.   Even in wild nature, in the case of trees and shrubs, and
of the large class of plants which we call weeds, it is only now
and then that we come upon finely grown specimens enjoying
the soil, and site, and air, precisely suited to their various needs.
One may live in a region where, walking five miles in any direction, and making the closest search, he can only find on the border
of a bit of woodland, among the brush between it and the edge
of a late-cleared field, a few score plants of the Fringed Gentian
pushing up their pretty blue flowers, in the early autumn, through
the tangle; and he may flatter himself that he knows something
of its habits.   But let him find himself among the meadows of
Berkshire, near Stockbridge or Lenox, and come by chance upon
one of the many sites in which the Gentian delights, and he will
hardly go back to his own starvelings again.   For, as he stands
upon the Berkshire hillside, he will see below him the wide
field all blue with the multitude of these flowers he has been
taught to think so shy, set thicker than the dandelions in early
spring, and the plants no pigmies either, such as he has been
accustomed to, with sometimes only one flower, and, at the most
with five or six, but giants three feet high, and with thirty, fifty,
sixty flowers apiece, counting them in all stages, from the half-
opened buds to those fully open, and with all the fringed cur-
tains of their eyes advanced.   Now he may well think he knows

what the Fringed Gentian really is; he has seen it growing as it was meant to grow. Who can say that he has fairly seen the Cardinal-flower, until he finds it unsought, thrown down by a marshy brookside, like a splendid scarlet carpet whereon, only a minute ago, Oberon and all his court were seated in merry play, but vanished at the sound of a human foot! Or golden rod, or dog-tooth violet, or the wild iris, or michaelmas daisy, or any of the sweet wilding brood; who knows them, till he finds them where they are of their own will, in a place in harmony with their genius? The botanist hunts far and wide, and questions every traveller, till he finds the real habitat of the plant he is studying; not the place where it can be made to grow, by forcing or coaxing, but the place it loves to grow in, the place it will crawl to, climb to, send out runners, roots, tendrils, winged seeds, to seek, and where, when it has once arrived, it will grow in all the glory it is capable of for a hundred years. The very sight of so vulgar a thing as a squash-vine crowning some ignoble dunghill, where it has been chance-sown, with its magnificent leafy crown, and sending out on every side its wild freebooter runners, now creeping close along the ground, cat-like, as if ready for a spring; now mounting the garden wall, now swinging up with one hand to the top of some low shed, and hiding it with its great cloak of leaves and golden flowers, and, perhaps, building up there, out of reach, the mighty globe that is to take the prize at the next county fair;—such a rude sight as this is inspiring in its way; we feel that we have seen one thing at least in creation doing, with all its might, the work it was intended to do. But, for the most part, rich people who have "places," and who have, what Job didn't have, a head-gardener; and people not rich, who have gardens that must, they think, be kept in order, rarely ever see any plant growing as it has a mind. Trees are pruned and cut back, grape-vines are duly pinched, strawberries are forbid to run, tomatoes are put in straight-waistcoats and kept down, and the whole garden, doubt-less for its own good, is trained to walk in the narrow road of duty. But, once let the head-gardener persecute his miserable employer up to that point beyond which endurance is not pos-sible to human nature, and be sent away, taking with him his whole corps of assistants, and, by the arts best known to the tribe, keeping his late master out of a successor for a month or two; or, let the family shut up the place, and go summering in other parts, and how these shrubs, flowers, and vegetables do behave, for all the pains spent on their education! See the fig-tree in the corner, struggling with the sweet-pea vines, and coming out second best! Look yonder, at the Maurandia that has made a thick curtain clean across the great window of the library, so that the servant, who tries to open the blinds from within, "can't think whatever do hold the d'ratted thing!" By Po-mona! those strawberries that we have forbid, over and over again, to get out of their beds, have slipped off, and, like Leigh Hunt's pig-driver's pig, "are running down all manner of streets!" The purslane has covered the walks with its pretty rosettes, the sorrel has filled every cranny with its sparkling tufts, the whole garden, in short, is a wilderness, in which all man's petty, useful laws and regulations are forgotten, and where the poet is as much delighted as the new head-gardener is dis-mayed.

As we have said already, an effort has been made to secure in the Ramble something of that flavor of wildness that gives the zest to a walk in the woods and open fields, and that makes the charm of some of the English and French country places. Absolute wildness is neither possible here, nor desirable, but enough of it, it was thought, could be seized and imprisoned to please the artist and the poet, with children, and all real lovers of simple nature. And it seems to us that the Com-missioners have succeeded, even better than could have been hoped, in freeing the Ramble from the appearance of artifice and restraint. It is not the real country, to be sure, but it is enough like it to give pleasure to those who know the country best, and the lover of flowers will find here many examples of the sort of culture we have been speaking of, by which he is enabled to judge how certain flowers that he has never seen growing except alone, or under the restraints of ordinary garden culture, look when planted in great numbers, in masses, and with no perceptible restraint at all. For ourselves, we have never seen in any private garden such a splendid display of rhodo-dendrons as may be witnessed every year in the Ramble, near the rustic arch and the Cave; we get but a poor idea of what the plant is from merely seeing it in a pot, or standing alone in the garden-bed. Then, there is our grandmother's favorite, the hydrangea. We always thought it a vapid flower, with its petals of no color, and ready to take any hue its owner may have the chemic skill to give them, but, since we have seen it massed along the slopes of the Terrace, we are ready to ad-mit that we had not done it justice, for it is a flower that, when properly treated, is capable of producing a charming effect. And, when the hydrangeas have had their turn, we hope that the Park gardener will let us see how hollyhocks will look in the place their paler rivals now occupy. It strikes us that this splendid plant is exactly suited to those sloping banks about the Terrace, both by its pyramidal form and by the magnificent color of its flowers. Its very formality, although in reality it is less formal than is sometimes represented, for its stalks often get blown down by the winds, or weighed down by heavy rains, and in the effort to right themselves, contrive to get twists and curves enough for picturesqueness,—but whatever formality it has, especially fits it for being planted near a piece of architecture like the Terrace, whose lines are almost all horizontal; while its masses of brilliant color, scarlet, rose-scarlet, crimson, purple-black, lemon-yellow, white, and rose, would relieve the monotonous tint of the stone, and set the building in a gorgeous frame. Up to this time, we believe, the Hollyhock has not been planted in the Park. It is despised by some people, and counted a poor man's flower, a country flower, not fit to grace any rich man's garden, much less so stately a place as this garden of the people. Here is an opportunity to teach these mistaken people a lesson they will be glad to learn. For no real lover of flowers could be insensible to such a sight as the gardener of the Park, with all the resources he has at his command, could show us, if he

INTERIOR OF MARBLE ARCH.

would, by planting on these terrace-banks, or along some alley of a hundred feet or so in length, and with a background of evergreens, groups of the finest hollyhocks from the recent prize shows in England, where this plant has long been a favorite, and where, under cultivation, it has attained an astonishing perfection both in the size and color of the flowers, and in profusion of bloom.

Those who frequent the Park must often have had occasion to thank the Commissioners for the abundance with which water is supplied in springs and wayside drinking fountains. The authorities have provided amply for the wants in this respect not only of men and horses, but of all the animals inhabiting the Park. We have already given an illustration of one out of the many drinking fountains to be met with under the various archways and bridges. Another will be found under the marble archway, a structure near the southern end of the Mall, which, from being a little off our road, we have not before spoken of. This is one of the pleasantest and most elegantly built of all these cool places for rest and refreshment. It is entered at one end on a level with the footpath; at the other a double stairway to left and right leads to the level of the Mall and to the carriage-road which this archway is designed to carry. It is called the *marble archway* to distinguish it, all the other structures of this sort in the Park being built either of stone, or brick, or of brick and stone combined. The marble employed is the coarse limestone from the Westchester quarries, which has been so largely used of late for building in New York City. The archway proper runs under the main carriage drive that nearly crosses the Park at this point and connects the two drives at either side running north and south. A marble bench runs along each side, and at the end, as is shown by our cut, a semicircular niche accommodates those who prefer the fuller light that reaches it from the stairway. In this niche there is to be placed a suitable marble basin with drinking-cups, but, at present, water is obtained from a common hydrant. The interior of this archway is peculiarly light and attractive, and far more cheerful than the other structures of a similar sort in the Park. Here, on a warm day, the children and their nurses gather with their luncheon-baskets, or the reader comes with his book and a sandwich, and whiles away a sultry hour at noon. Over the railing of the bridge above we well remember leaning one Fourth of July evening, watching the

slow sunset fade, and after, far into the night, along the wide
horizon

—" break
The rocket molten into flakes
Of crimson or in emerald rain."

The elevation here is just sufficient to enable one to know that
he is surrounded by a city, without looking down upon it.   A
little beyond the marble arch, and near the Seventh Avenue, is
the bridge shown in our next cut, where, as in all the passages
of this kind in the Park, there are seats along the walls and a
drinking fountain.   This bridge is built of red Philadelphia
brick and a yellow brick, probably from Milwaukee, arranged

BRIDGE OF RED AND YELLOW BRICK NEAR THE SEVENTH AVENUE.

in alternate stripes, the red bricks, beside, being set at an angle
instead of flush, a disposition which proves quite decorative in
effect, giving shadow, taking off from the bald appearance of
mere stripes, and making the contrast of color more value.   The
arch of this bridge is supported externally at the ends by cut
granite quoins and keystones, and the red and yellow bands of
the outside are continued within.

But the needed refreshment of water is not always supplied
in these artificial ways. In many places in the Park, not only
in the Ramble but in the upper park, in the Ravine, and here
and there lower down along the western side, we come upon
pretty natural springs like this in our cut, where the water

SPRING NEAR EIGHTH AVENUE.

wells out from the living rock and is set in a frame of leafage
as every spring should be by rights. Many a time in our walks
have we come upon some little bird taking his bath in the pool
that receives the falling water, nor has he always thought it
necessary to fly away at our approach. Near the restaurant

at Mount St. Vincent there has lately been constructed an extremely pretty spring. The water flows gently down over the face of a nearly perpendicular rock, keeping it always moist, but not flowing with too full a stream to forbid the growth of mosses and ferns in the slight ledges along its face, and is received at the bottom in a deep tank. This spring has been arranged expressly for horses, and is on the horseback-ride near the pretty cedarn arbor, seen from the road just before reaching the restaurant. In the upper part of the Park, where rocks of this description are quite common, other rustic springs similar to the one which we have just described, are to be constructed from time to time, so that when the laying out of the grounds is completed there will be, in every part, abundant provision of water for man and beast. And it is pleasant to remember that, thus far at least, all the water that is in the Park, excepting, of course, the two Croton Reservoirs, whether it be in the form of lakes or pools, brooks, fountains, or springs, is the natural product of the ground, not borrowed from the outside country. The water that used to stagnate in these marshes, or to creep lazily along in slender streams, half choked with duckweed and cress, has been thus transformed by the skill of the engineers and landscape gardeners, and made to minister both to use and beauty.

We have often alluded to the animals that have their pleasant home in the Park; of those which are permitted to run at large the Ramble offers to many a delightful shelter, where they may almost forget the nearness of the city. Indeed, if it were not for dogs, which, although forbidden in the Park, will often make an entry by night, and do mischief in spite of all precautions, there is no danger, or there would be none if the wall and gates were completed, in allowing the deer to roam at will. But neither the wall nor the gates would be a sufficient protection against dogs, if the deer and sheep were unguarded, and the former, therefore, are confined to their enclosures, and the latter intrusted to the care and crook of their faithful shepherd. In the Ramble, then, we can only study the habits in freedom of certain birds, unless it be those of the rabbits, wild and tame, but the company of these we can really enjoy, for they are evidently at home, and have learned, by this time, to be quite fearless in the presence of visitors. Among the fowls, too, the good old English of our Bible allows us to reckon the bees, which, somewhere, are called " the smallest of the fowl," and an in-fant colony of these little creatures is fairly domesticated here, hav-ing its huts under the pretty shelter which we show in our cut. Pro-bably there would be more of these if it were not that the bees are such troublesome crea-tures to manage, and

BEE-HIVE IN RAMBLE.

that in the course of a year a great many children would be stung by them. If they were not almost as fearful wild-fowl as Bottom's lion, being not only constitutionally irritable, but whimsical, which is worse; apt to fly into a passion at an ill smell, prone to fall out with people not sufficiently given to bathing, and, on the other hand, like enough to persecute any lady carrying a scented handkerchief, or with perfumed hair, to her peril;—it would be a very pleasant addition to the attractions of the Park to have an opportunity of studying the operations of bees in their hives. Many a delightful hour might be passed, surveying

"The singing masons building roofs of gold,"

that is if they would let us, but, as is well known, the bees like

BIRD-HOUSE IN RAMBLE.

to keep their doings to themselves, and if the glass by which we watch them remain long uncovered, they will make a waxen screen, and shut out prying eyes.

The English sparrows however, for whom these picturesque houses are being built in various parts of the Park, beside the Ramble, are by no means so shy, nor, to us humans, so ill-disposed, although they are pugnacious little fellows and fight forever among themselves. But they are such brisk, tight-bodied, chirruping, bright-eyed chaps, that, after brief acquaintance with them, we expect to see them do every thing,—fighting, love-making, eating, and drinking, with as much fuss and fury as possible. They picked up these manners, we suppose, in England, and they look like Englishmen in miniature, for all the world! We happened to be in the Park on St. Valentine's Day, and there was a hubbub, to be sure! The sparrows may have called it "wooing," but it looked to us like a general scrimmage. Such scolding and chattering, such hard blows given and taken, such chipper defiance, and hot pursuit on the least provocation! It was as noisy as a political caucus, and sounded wonderfully like swearing! They are industrious little creatures, however, and not only the Central Park, but the whole city, is greatly in their debt for the thorough way in which they keep the measuring-worms down. Visitors to the Park must have noticed how free the trees are from destructive insects and worms; a caterpillar's nest is a thing not to be seen there, and we suppose that a great deal of this freedom from what, in many parts of our city, had grown to be a real nuisance, is owing to the freedom that birds of all kinds enjoy here. They pay for all the care that is taken to protect their lives, and make them comfortable.

The pea-fowl are the most attractive residents of the Ramble, and they seem to find life there very agreeable. They may often be seen on the lawns on sunny days: the cocks stepping majestically about, with their magnificent trains, and the meek hens following them, their quiet-colored plumage serving as a foil to the splendid hues in which their lords are arrayed. Now and then, apparently from no other motive than pure whim, the male will vouchsafe the world a sight of his outspread tail, and if he succeeds in attracting a sufficiently large crowd of children with their nurses, and is greeted by enough flattering "ohs!" and "ahs!" he will complacently turn himself about to the right and left for twenty minutes or so, apparently under the impression that the entire Park, and the whole world, for that matter, was created expressly as a platform and background for the display of his splendor. It is, by no means, uncommon either, for him to be so carried away by the extreme admiration bestowed upon him, as to fancy that he can add, as it were, a perfume to the violet, by lifting his voice in song, but the first few notes of his raucous and discordant cry are generally sufficient to disperse the assembly in most admired disorder, the infants adding their squalls to his, and the nurses, terrified out of their wits, snatching up their charges, and seeking refuge from the beautiful monster in the nearest summer-house.

For ourselves, we better like to come upon the peacocks when they are lying at ease in some covert, say in the late autumn days, among the withered leaves, where, at first, they are not

LAWN IN RAMBLE WITH PEA-FOWL.

perceived, but presently, all at once, the eye catches the unwonted gleam of the neck with its indescribable green-blue, such as nothing in nature can rival, except the hues and lights of certain precious stones. Other birds, indeed, and some of the South American butterflies and beetles, have colors as splendid, but they are distributed in much smaller masses, or on smaller bodies. No other bird, we believe, is at once so large as the peacock and so gorgeously arrayed. His beauty is proverbial, particularly among the Eastern nations, and beside making use of his plumage in various decorative manufacture, they often employ its markings and colors in their designs, imitating its hues with stained mother-of-pearl, and with lapis, emerald, and turquoise. He plays an important part too in the Mohammedan legends, and, perhaps, the reader may not object to hearing how the Arab prophet introduced him among the personages concerned in the great drama of the Fall of Man.

Allah himself said to Adam and Eve, "I have appointed this garden for your abode, it will shelter you from cold and heat, from hunger and thirst. Take, at your discretion, of every thing that it contains; only one of its fruits shall be denied you. Beware that ye transgress not this one command, and watch against the wily rancor of Iblis! He is your enemy, because he was overthrown on your account; his cunning is infinite, and he aims at your destruction."

The newly-created pair attended to Allah's words, and lived a long time, some say five hundred years, in Paradise without approaching the forbidden tree. But Iblis also had listened to Allah, and resolving to lead man into sin, wandered constantly in the outskirts of heaven, seeking to glide unobserved into Paradise. But its gates were shut, and guarded by the angel Ridwhan. One day the peacock came out of the garden. He was the finest of the birds of Paradise, for his plumage shone like the pearl and emerald, and his voice was so melodious that he was appointed to sing the praises of Allah daily in the main street of heaven.

Iblis, on seeing him, said to himself, "Doubtless this beautiful bird is very vain; perhaps I may be able to induce him, by flattery, to bring me secretly into the garden."

When the peacock had gone so far from the gate that he could no longer be overheard by Ridwhan, Iblis said to him:—

"Most wonderful and beautiful bird! art thou of the birds of Paradise?"

"I am: but who art thou, who seemest frightened, as if some one did pursue thee?"

"I am one of those cherubim who are appointed to sing, without ceasing, the praises of Allah, but have glided away for an instant to visit the Paradise which He has prepared for the faithful. Wilt thou conceal me under thy beautiful wings?"

"Why should I do an act which must bring the displeasure of Allah upon me?"

"Take me with thee, charming bird, and I will teach thee three mysterious words, which shall preserve thee from sickness, age, and death."

"Must, then, the inhabitants of Paradise die?"

"All, without exception, who know not the three words which I possess."

"Speakest thou the truth?"

"By Allah, the Almighty!"

The peacock believed him, for he did not even dream that any creature would swear falsely by its maker; yet, fearing lest Ridwhan might search him too closely on his return, he steadily refused to take Iblis along with him, but promised to send out the serpent, who might more easily discover the means of introducing him unobservedly into the garden.

Now the serpent was at first the queen of all beasts. Her head was like rubies, and her eyes like emerald. Her skin shone like a mirror of various hues. Her hair was soft like that of a noble virgin; and her form resembled the stately camel; her breath was sweet like musk and amber, and all her words were songs of praise. She fed on saffron, and her resting-places were on the blooming borders of the beautiful river Cantharus. She was created a thousand years before Adam, and destined to be the playmate of Eve.

The rest of the legend need not be given. The peacock so

frightens the beautiful and luxurious serpent with the idea of death, that she straightway runs out of the garden, and is easily persuaded by Iblis to allow him to enter Paradise hid in the hollow of one of her teeth. As a punishment for his complicity in the crime of Iblis, the peacock was condemned to lose his beautiful voice, and, on being expelled from Paradise, was ordered to take up his abode in Persia. In these later years he has exchanged the rose-gardens of Persia for haunts farther west, and has long since become a familiar bird with us. No less than seventy-nine are domesticated in the Park, and, of these, the greater number are to be met with in the Ramble.

LAWN IN RAMBLE WITH GUINEA-FOWL.

Belonging to the same sub-order as the pea-fowl, but less striking in appearance, are the guinea-fowl, of which the Park possesses one hundred and fifty-four specimens. The majority of these are of the well-known gray variety, there being only two of the far less common, white. The guinea-fowl is much shyer than his more showy relative, and will not remain so quietly to be watched, but it is pretty if one can come unawares upon the parents, leading about their tiny speckled brood. If they spy us, however, they quickly take themselves to cover. One wonders if the Arabs have a fable ready to account for the harsh voice which these birds share with their cousins, the peafowl; probably it was only thought necessary to account for the discrepancy between the elegant shape and brilliant coloring of the larger bird, and his horrible voice, while contrast between the sober gray and rather clumsy shape of the guineafowl, and his rough cry, was so much less striking as to pass

FREDERICK LAW OLMSTED.

with little notice. Mr. Bellows was so fortunate as to find a party of these birds so intent upon making havoc among the grasshoppers on the lawn as to be entirely unconscious of the fact, that "a chiel was amang 'em takin' notes," until he had them safely down, in their native gray and white.

Less familiar than these birds, but hardly less interesting, are several strangers, from far-away parts of our own country or from over-seas, which we shall meet in any of our strolls through the Ramble, and of which we have already spoken. Many of our readers will have made the acquaintance long ago of the Heron who wanders about for the present without a mate, but who will doubtless find his Eve advancing toward him out of the rushes some fine morning, when some philanthropic person shall have presented her to the Commissioners. The same good

CALVERT VAUX.

service will also have to be done for the Stork, who, in the absence of his wife, has forsworn all society, and devotes himself exclusively to solving the problem, how long he can stand on one leg, with his bill buried in his breast-feathers, so that he presents the appearance of a lady's summer parasol stuck on end in the sod, and waiting for an owner. The two Tiger Bitterns are more sociable, and seem to have some business in the

world, but their manners are too stately, their steps too meas-
ured, and their way of looking at us out of the side of their
eye too chilling and critical that we should feel any lively interest in them. The company of the lively little sparrows is a
vast deal more entertaining.

Beside the living animals that either wander at will in the
Park, and enjoy life after their several fashions, or are shut up
in the temporary cages that have been provided for them until
the grounds and buildings of the Zoological Gardens shall be
ready, the Commissioners have laid the foundation of a collection of stuffed animals, and have already placed a considerable
number of specimens in the halls of the Arsenal. Since we began to write the present account this building has been almost
entirely remodeled, and already presents a very different appearance externally from that which it has in the earlier sketches
by Mr. Bellows. The central part of the building has been
raised a story, and the eight towers have been covered with low-
pitched, eight-sided roofs. Any slight suggestion of a military
purpose which the edifice may have had a year ago, has thus
been obliterated, and the interior has, beside, been fitted up to
serve better than it used to do the purposes of a museum, and
to give better accommodation to the offices of the Commission.
In passing, we may mention that on one of the floors a large
room at the north end of the building has been appropriated to
meteorological observations and investigations, under the immediate direction of a gentleman who, if appearances go for any
thing, is, undoubtedly, the original Clerk of the Weather. It
really gives one a romantic shock, so to speak, to leave the gay
drives and walks of the Park, all alive with stylish teams, and
turn-outs of the latest rig, with crowds of people dressed in
the very height of the fashion of to-day, and to climb to this
lofty room, whose windows command, not only all this festive
show, a round of gala-days, but miles and miles, beside, of mod-

ern wealth and splendor, and to find here this little old-time gentleman just stepped out of the Waverly Novels—a very Dominie Sampson—begging his pardon, with his queer little queue, his powdered hair, his knee-breeches, and worsted stockings, and low-cut, silver-buckled shoes, and, better still, an old-time courtesy of manners such as one rarely meets in these scurvy days! Here, all day, and, doubtless, all night, too, for that matter, he lives among his multitude of instruments, and watches with unwearied vigilance the whims and vagaries of his thermometers, barometers, and rain-gauges, and takes note of all Nature's doings with his telescopes, microscopes, and the whole staff of mechanical detectives, with which we ingenious humans have surrounded the ancient Dame, who must, by this time, have begun to despair of ever getting a chance to work in secret again. The Commissioners have, it seems to us, done a very good thing in establishing this miniature Observatory in the Park, and in default of an establishment such as ought surely to be found in a city of the size of New York, and would be, if our fellow-citizens were not so wholly, so fatally, absorbed in the one pursuit of money-getting and money-spending, this may serve as a valuable adjunct to institutions much more pretending. Here has been established a system of regular meteorological observations, comprising barometrical, thermometrical, and hygrometrical observations, as also those showing the force and direction of the winds, and other atmospheric phenomena. The report of the Commission for the year 1867, contained a series of tables showing the results obtained by these observations, on such points as—"The heights of the barometer, monthly, during the year 1867." "The state of the thermometer, monthly." "The durations and depths of rain and snow, monthly." "The number of igneous meteors observed, monthly." "The number of luminous meteors, monthly;" and, lastly, "The number of thunder storms, monthly," and the days on which they occurred.

These observations are made useful to the general public by being published at certain regular intervals in the principal city journals and scientific periodicals, as well as in the annual Reports of the Commission.

In the other stories of the Arsenal are the few stuffed animals which have thus far been presented to the Park, and those of the living animals in cages which cannot well bear the exposure to the open air. The stronger animals, the various foxes, the black bears, the prairie-dogs, and the eagles, are in the yard on the east side of the building. Within, we find a collection already extremely interesting, and sure to become more so when proper provision shall have been made for the reception of animals that will hereafter be presented. New York, after talking the matter over for nearly fifty years, has, at last, taken the first steps toward the formation of a proper Zoological Garden, and there is every reason to hope that the next Report of the Commission may assure us that it is no longer a dream but an accomplished fact. And it will be interesting to note that when we get it, it will prove to be owing directly to the stimulus given by the Park authorities to the public desire and curiosity to see and study the animal world—a curiosity as old as the oldest man—for Adam was hardly more than created before he began to study the animals about him, and give them names! From the time when a few cages and enclosed slips of lawn near the Mall were appropriated to the score or two of birds, monkeys, and deer, then owned by the Park, it has been evident that nothing could be shown to the people more sure to gratify them, than a fine collection of animals, domestic and foreign. This was the beginning of the new enthusiasm for a Zoological Garden, and by the securing of Manhattan Square, on the western side of the Eighth Avenue, between Seventy-seventh and Eighty-first streets, the only real obstacle, namely, want of room, has been removed, to our having what so many other great cities have long enjoyed, a complete garden of animals. Nor do we despair of seeing set up in the Arsenal, or in some place more suitable, a series of aquarial cases, salt water and fresh, as fine as that which used to redeem Barnum's Museum from the reproach of total vulgarity, and elevated it, indeed, to the rank, in that regard, of a real scientific institution. After all, to establish a collection of aquaria even more complete than that, would be by no means a difficult undertaking for the Commissioners, and there would be no reason for its not being made a source of revenue to the Park by the sale of small cases containing collections suited to beginners, or of the surplus of specimens that might be on hand at the end of the year. The Park sells the sheep, the hay, the white mice that it does not want; why should it not be allowable to quote the income derived from stickle-backs, sea-anemones, and hermit-crabs?

These sea-gardens are, however, things of the future; meanwhile, the Commissioners are about to take advantage of a rare opportunity to enrich the Park with a collection of models of the extinct Fauna, more particularly of those that once inhabited this Continent. No doubt, some of our readers have visited in England the gardens of the Sydenham Crystal Palace, and have been surprised, delighted, it may be frightened, on coming, entirely unprepared, upon the models of extinct animals, which were constructed, perhaps ten years ago, for the proprietors of that wonderful museum, by Mr. Waterhouse Hawkins, a gentleman well known, now in New York, by his remarkable lectures on geology and the antediluvians, delivered in this city during the winter of 1867-8. "Who that has seen them can ever forget the feelings with which, on coming out from the narrow, tunnel-like cut in the rocks, he suddenly found himself face to face, first with one and then with another, of the gigantic reptiles and quadrupeds that made the ancient world hideous. Perhaps he had read of these monsters with eager curiosity in Cuvier, or Lyell, or Mantell, or had seen in the British Museum, or elsewhere, their fossil remains, wonderful to look at, however crushed or dislocated or incomplete. But here, at Sydenham, he stood in their very presence, and received for the first time, a living impression of what these creatures really were. And if he stayed long enough to study them, he must have come away with a new interest in geology, and with a feeling of indebtedness to the clever and learned man who had re-created these extinct beings for him, out of the scattered remains that are left of them."* Mr. Hawkins, as we have said, has been engaged to perform the same good office for us that he has already performed for England, and it will not be long before we shall have the pleasure of looking at the express images of the Mastadon, Megatherium, Plesiosaurus, and Iguanodon, as they lived, and moved, and had their mighty beings, in the far away dusk of the primeval ages. Just where they are to be placed we do not know; perhaps the Commission has not yet fully decided where they can be most advantageously built up— ay, "built up," that is the word, for these are to be structures, edifices, buildings! Nothing less than brick, mortar, stones, and timbers can be employed to construct creatures beside whom the largest of living quadrupeds, reptiles, or birds would have looked pigmy and starved. But whatever place may be fixed upon, we hope that it will be one, as nearly as possible, resembling that in the Sydenham Gardens, where the surroundings may assist the imagination of the spectator in taking in the idea of these monsters and their relations to the actual earth. They will not, we trust, be put under cover, or placed on pedestals, or in any way made a formal show of. Half their effect, we may almost say half their usefulness will be destroyed if they are not given a

* Putnam's Monthly, *June*. 1868.

habitat, as near as may be, like the one they enjoyed while in the flesh. When Mr. Hawkins has brought us into the very presence where—

> "Behemoth, biggest born of earth, upheaves
> His vastness,"

surrounded by all the giant brood that, happily for man, are long since vanished from his world; and when the long promised Zoological Gardens, and the hoped-for Aquaria shall have been completed, we shall have in our own New York a worthy rival to the famous institutions of London and Paris, the Zoological Gardens and the Jardin des Plantes, and it will be our own fault if they do not, in time, become as famous as their models.

As we have several times alluded to the gates of the Park, perhaps this will be as good an opportunity as we shall find, to speak of this important subject. Up to this time, owing to the condition of the grades of the two avenues, the Eighth and the Fifth, it has been considered advisable by the Commissioners that as little as possible should be done in the matter of the enclosing walls of the Park, and that the whole subject of the gates giving access to the interior should be postponed until those grades shall have been irrevoeably fixed, and the walls themselves in an advanced state of completion. But, even if we did not know the fact to have been so, it would not require any very profound knowledge of human nature to predict that a general impatience would be felt at the prolonged postponement of the gateways, or that a strong effort would be made to force the public to accept the design of some ambitious individual. No doubt the patience of the Commissioners has been severely tried in the effort to resist both public and private importunity, and thanks are due them for this evidence, as for so many others, of their determination to refuse their consent to any proposition that, in their judgment, would not serve the real interests of the public in the Park.

"In the month of June, 1863, the Board, by advertisements in the newspapers, offered a premium of five hundred dollars for the best set of designs for the four gateways in the southern boundary of the Park. In answer to the offer of the Board, twenty-one designs were submitted, no one of which, after examination, seemed to the Board calculated fully to meet the expectations of the public, though several of them presented features of merit. None of them were accepted, and the premium-money was directed to be divided among the competitors; subsequently, sketches for the four southerly gateways of the southerly boundary of the Park were approved, in their general features, and their erection authorized." These few words in their Seventh Annual Report (1863), contain the only allusion ever publicly made by the Commissioners to a subject which gave rise, at the time, to no small amount of newspaper controversy, and to, at least, one book of considerable pretensions.

The sketches alluded to in the paragraph quoted above, were made by Mr. Richard M. Hunt, an architect of this city. His designs were accepted by the Commissioners too hastily, owing to a pressure from the public for the erection of gates of some kind, and to a pressure from within, for the erection of these gates in particular. For we are sure that no deliberate and unprejudiced study of them could ever have resulted in their being accepted. Without going into details of criticism, it may be enough to say, that they were entirely out of keeping with every thing else in the Park; that they called for extensive and costly changes in the grades, and in the laying out of the surface of the Park directly about them; and that they were all dependent for any effect or beauty they were expected to have, upon statuary, which, being cheap upon paper, was largely used by the designer, but which would have made them, supposing the best sculptors to have been employed, expensive beyond all bounds of reason. Apart from the sculpture heaped upon them, they had nothing to recommend them to an educated taste, and very little to catch even the popular eye.

While the Commission itself might have been divided upon this subject, there was found to be very little division in the minds of the public, when the designs were presented to them for criticism. A certain popular feeling manifested itself, as well by the public silence, as by any pointed or spoken speech, against the adoption of these designs, and the Commissioners, feeling this plainly enough, determined to wait until they could be satisfied that the most intelligent public opinion would authorize them in carrying out their first intention. They waited, therefore, and this delay was fatal to Mr. Hunt's aspirations. After every opinion that was offered to the Board, in public or in private, had been examined, there could be but one result discovered— a decree of condemnation, and the Commissioners, considering themselves the servants of the public, decided to leave the whole matter where it was before their call for a competition in 1863. In 1865—May 11th—at a meeting of the Board, it was formally resolved, "That all work on the gateways of the Park be deferred till the further order of the Board." And this officially closed the whole matter as between Mr. Hunt, the Commissioners, and the public.

It is, of course, to be desired that, as soon as is possible, the boundary-wall of the Park should be completed, and gates set up at all the entrances. But we venture to hope that the good taste thus far shown by the architects of the Park, and by the Commission will not fail them at this important stage of the work, and that in the future, as in the past, they will be strong enough to avoid every thing savoring of ostentation, affectation,

or mere vulgar display of ornaments and decorative features with
nothing behind, or beneath them, of use. There ought, in our
opinion, to be two principal gates on the southern boundary-
line: one at the southeast angle—Fifth Avenue and Fifty-ninth
Street; the other at the southwest angle—Fifty-ninth Street and
Eighth Avenue. The first of them is the one to which the
Commissioners have given the name of the Scholars' Gate; the
second is to be known as the Merchants' Gate. The point
chosen for the Scholars' Gate is distinctly marked by its neighborhood to the pretty "Pond," as it is called, to distinguish it

POND NEAR THE SCHOLARS' GATE.

from the larger sheet of water near the Terrace named the Lake.
The Merchants' Gate is at present indicated by the bronze statue
of Commerce, of which we have already spoken. At both these
points the ground has been so shaped and graded as to afford
most favorable positions for gates as dignified, and as richly
decorated, as the city can afford. But this cannot be said of
the greater number of the entrances, nor is it desirable that the
gates should all be equally magnificent or expensive. For our
part, we confess that we have an objection to the expending of

a great deal of thought, or a great deal of money, upon mere gateways. Decorative design, as Ruskin has so well shown, belongs to places where men rest, where they have leisure and opportunity to enjoy it. The same law that orders decoration, especially such as is delicately minute, to be placed on the lower stories of buildings where it can be studied and enjoyed, dictates that it should not be wasted on places whose very purpose forbids that we should pause in them long enough to appreciate the artist's skill, or to penetrate his thought. Such a place is a gateway, which, while it ought, no doubt, to be distinctly marked and defined, ought rather to make upon the mind some single impression of grandeur or beauty, than to call for a stay in one's walk or drive sufficiently long to study, and understand, and enjoy, the minute beauties of its design. There is always, perhaps, a certain pleasure in passing under a lofty arch of beautiful form, and gateways of this description admit of great variety of design, with the addition of whatever statuary may be thought suitable. But, after all, the gateway itself ought to be the important thing; it should be both effective and useful, should have evidently something more than a merely ornamental part to play, and should especially avoid any thing looking like an encouragement to loafers, and idle people generally, to linger about it, staring and gazing in listless curiosity. The one use of a gate is to afford ingress and egress. It may be made, to a certain degree, commemorative or monumental, but, so sure as we attempt to make it either of these first, and merely useful, last, we shall have a result that will be less and less satisfactory to the public, as good taste becomes more and more extended and confirmed.

We can either leave the Ramble on the east by descending the steps cut in the Belvedere rock, and keeping to the left, by doing which we shall come out at the stone carriage-step where we entered; or by taking the path that runs along the very edge of the Reservoir, between it and the traffic-road that tunnels the hill at this point. Reaching the southeastern angle of the Reservoir, we descend rapidly, and find ourselves passing across a wide and little-broken tract lying between the Reservoir and the Fifth Avenue. This lawn-like expanse is crossed only by the carriage-road and the bridle-path, which, at one point, passes under the drive by a very pretty archway, lined with buff and red bricks, and with picturesque entrances of brown stone. Up to within a year or two of the present time the Reservoir on this side has been· particularly unsightly, there being nothing to hide its bare and roughly constructed wall with the plain picket-fence running along the top. But the trees that were early planted against it are now well grown, and, in 1866, the Croton Board, relaxing a little in their love of the stiff, good-naturedly consented to cut the picket-fence down to a less awkwardly conspicuous height, and even if the Board should not think well of the notion of putting a stone railing of agreeable form in place of the picket-fence, we may hope that nature will soon show her entire want of sympathy with these matter-of-fact people by running a beautiful Gothic sky-line of tree-tops just above the monotonous pickets. This is the only device that can be relied on for escape from these eyesores, for it is too much to hope that the Reservoir itself will ever be done away with, and, so long as it stands, it is, of course, a thing only to be endured, and, as much as possible, to be hid.

Near the northeast angle of the Reservoir, in a triangular plot formed by its wall with the foot-path and the third traffic-road, is to be placed "The Maze," which will, no doubt, be a very popular amusement for children, for whose use it has been especially contrived. Yet, after all, there was a time, and that a very pleasant one, too, when grown-up people enjoyed being puzzled by a Maze, and when no place of any pretensions to size and grandeur was without one. This was in Anne's time and those of the first Georges', and, indeed, the fashion continued down to the beginning of the century. Cowper, who wrote upon any thing and every thing, and whose verse enshrines so many of the fashionable follies of the day, like flies in amber, made this trifle, probably at the call of some one of his many friends:—

THE MAZE.

From right to left, and to and fro,
Caught in a labyrinth, you go,
And turn, and turn, and turn again
To solve the mystery, but in vain;
Stand still and breathe, and take from me
A clew that soon shall set you free!
Not Ariadne, if you met her,
Herself could serve you with a better.
You entered easily—find where—
And make, with ease, your exit there!

At this point, the foot-path strikes into the carriage-road, and both together make a rapid curve to the east, in order to reach the extremely narrow space that lies between the new Reservoir and the Fifth Avenue, and gives access to the upper park. Here, too, the drive crosses the third traffic-road, which, passing between the two Reservoirs, and following the curving southern side of the new one, is the least direct in its course of all the four, issuing on the Fifth Avenue at Eighty-fifth Street, and on Eighth Avenue at Eighty-sixth Street. At the point where the carriage-drive crosses the traffic-road, a flight of steps with platforms leads to the foot-path that runs round the new Reservoir. As this structure covers an area of one hundred and six acres, stretching very nearly from one side of the Park to the other, it would have been a serious drawback to the beauty and usefulness of the Park as a pleasure-ground, if there had been no means of enjoying the sight of this great sheet of water. But

a foot-path has been carried round the entire circuit of this inland sea, and the bridle-road also runs round it, though at a
somewhat lower level than the foot-path, in places. It will be
seen, on referring to the Plan, that the bridle-road, after striking
directly across the Park at a point nearly opposite the Arsenal,
and passing three times under the main drive, continues in a
winding course up the western side of the Park, between the
main drive and the Eighth Avenue, until it reaches the northwestern angle of the smaller Reservoir. Here it divides to right
and left, completely encircling the new Reservoir, as we have
said, and, excepting in one or two places where it dips, commanding a view of the water all the way. On the northern
side of the Reservoir there are three points where this circuit
can be left for the lower level, and it can also be left or entered,
directly, at the Engineers' Gate—Fifth Avenue and Ninetieth
Street. At either end of the Reservoir—if a structure so irregular in outline may be said to have ends at all—we come upon
the two water-gates by which the in-flow and out-flow of the
stream is regulated. These gates are very conspicuous, and,
also, very ugly. If they were plain, four-square structures with
ordinary pitched roofs, and mere unornamented openings for
windows and doors, there would have been no particular fault
to find with them, and if we could not, in that case more than
this, call them handsome, at least we could not call them ugly.
Ugliness is never a mere negation, it is always positive; and
these gate-houses are ugly because they pretend to be decorative; they offend by what they have, not by what they want.
Up to this time, engineers all the world over have practically
insisted on the necessity of a complete divorce between usefulness and beauty. Brought up on the geometry of the schools, the
geometry of rule and compass, they are not aware, that is, they
act as if they were not aware, that there is any other sort of
geometry in existence. Yet it may safely be asserted that while

there is no such thing as a straight line in nature, the edges of crystals alone excepted, there is also no such thing on the surface of the earth as an object bounded or marked with accurate geometric curves; the nearest approach to an exception with which we are acquainted being the involutions of certain shells. Scientifically, this may be reckoned a loose statement, because, of course, every curve whatsoever is capable of being reduced to geometric laws, but we mean to say that all natural curves are with great difficulty reducible to geometric rules, and that nature, to speak with familiarity, draws with eye and hand, not with line and compass. And, again, it is a universal law, that nature's beauty is never extraneous, that her ornamentation is always structural; and it is capable of proof upon proof, that all enduring beauty in human work, and all the best ornament in that work, of whatever age, has followed nature's law in this, and been structural, not applied: in the nature of the thing, not in any outside and removable shell or covering.

Now the engineer has not been educated to think it necessary to consider "beauty" in designing his buildings, and if, in a moment of weakness, he is seized with a desire to rival the artist, and consents to try what he can do to make his work decorative, he is sure to produce some such result as we see in these new Reservoir gate-houses, where the stumpy corner-turrets are meant to be purely decorative, serving no useful purpose whatever. Now, until engineers can be brought, by education, to see that there is no antagonism between use and *real* beauty, we, for our part, would much prefer that they should hold closely to their utilitarian theory, and continue to swear by straight lines, circles, and arcs of circles, and even, if they like, to deny the existence of beauty altogether. But we cannot help thinking that the day must come when engineers, architects, and artists everywhere, will strike hands, and works of great public utility will no longer necessarily conflict with the higher utility of being at one with nature, and helping, not thwarting, the spiritual needs of man. We think there is good reason for complaint when a beautiful landscape is seriously marred by the erection of some useful building, or other structure, whose engineer has considered the landscape as a matter of no concern whatever. The tubular bridge over the Menai Strait, although not a work of absolute necessity, may be admitted a useful work, but all travellers of taste and feeling are agreed that it is one of the ugliest structures in existence, and by its size and conspicuous position, a great deformity in the landscape. We maintain that there was no need of this, that if the engineers who contrived it had been educated as engineers some day will be, they would have thought out the problem with an instinct for beauty as strong in them as the instinct for science, and made the Menai Bridge as lovely as Salisbury Spire. Indeed, the greatest engineers the world has ever seen were the Gothic architects of the thirteenth and fourteenth centuries; they solved the problem of combining use and beauty perfectly, and their buildings are equally wonderful, whether we study their construction or their ornamentation. This talk of ours, the reader will please remember, is taking place in front of the Engineers' Gate, and therefore cannot be objected to as *malapropos*. Nor would we be thought ungrateful to the engineers of the Central Park who have done here a vast deal of thorough and intelligent work, much of which is hid from the public eye, and can only be valued at its worth by those who look deeper than the surface.

The road that runs along the eastern side of the new Reservoir is planted on each side with a double row of trees, which have already made a fine growth, and, in time, this part of the main drive will pleasantly match the Mall, which it even now resembles. The Commissioners had, here, a real difficulty to surmount, and they have done it cleverly, as we have already seen them do many things in other parts of the Park. The problem was, to use to the best advantage the extremely narrow and elongated space between the new Reservoir and the Fifth Avenue. The whole width between the eastern edge of the Reservoir coping and the Park wall, is two hundred feet, and the length of road running along the Reservoir on this side is, as near as we can make it, two thousand feet. The space is, thus, by no means well proportioned, yet, in it, the Commissioners have secured a foot-path, a bridle-road, and the extremely pretty carriage-drive over which we are now trotting leisurely behind our imaginary team. The foot-path we have already alluded to; it runs close around the edge of the water, only separated from it by the coping of cut stone with its iron railing. The round of this Reservoir makes an admirable "constitutional;" the walk is in good order in almost all weather, and a fine breeze is pretty sure to be stirring up here, no matter how calm it may be below. So large a body of water may generally be reckoned on for waves of its own, and occasionally we have had the pleasure of being well dashed with spray. The wind has to be high, however, to accomplish this. From all points, the view is fine, and it is a glorious place from which to see sunsets. Many a time have we taken this walk for no other end but to enjoy the evening sky, and we must always have cheerful memories of a place that, after weary days spent in the dirty city, has so often lifted us into an atmosphere where all unpleasant experiences were, for a time, forgotten. Next to the foot-path but not, like it, always on one level, runs the bridle-path, also encircling the Reservoir. Midway on this eastern side, it can be left for the carriage-road, or for the Engineers' Gate, and there are several other places where it can be left or entered at the horseman's pleasure. Our narrow space of four hundred feet has, thus far, generously accommodated two paths: the remainder is occupied by the carriage-drive. This portion of the drive it was necessary to make perfectly straight, and it is the only place in the Park where the

Commissioners have not been able to avoid putting temptation in the way of the owners of fast horses. Fast driving is not only forbidden by the rules, but the roads have everywhere been laid out with such curves as to rob racing of its charms. Here, however, is a smooth, level, excellently paved course of two thousand feet in length, and it is not to be wondered at that men who own trotters are, every little while, found unable to resist the temptation to defy the Commissioners and let their horses try their mettle. The police in this part of the Park has to be constantly on the alert, and the crop of arrested Jehus is always fine in this quarter. In four years, 1863–66, the number arrested for fast driving was somewhat greater than that of those arrested for all other offences put together, being as 232 to 209, although this was not a very large number when all the temptations to disobedience are taken into account. In truth, the arrests in the Park, taken altogether, are much fewer than would be expected, and it would seem by the reports that they decrease yearly in proportion to the whole number of visitors; at all events, they do not increase. Thus, in 1866, the arrests were only in the proportion of 1 to about 75,000 visitors, while in 1867, the proportion was only 1 to about 60,000. Those ar- rested for fast driving are immediately taken before the nearest magistrate by the policeman making the arrest, and are fined, off-hand, ten dollars. It is gratifying to be able to state that the magistrates, almost without exception, stand by the Park authorities, and when the offence is proved, exact the fine with- out fear or favor. In New York, where justice is administered almost exclusively as a reward for agreement in political opin- ions with the judge, or as a punishment for political differences, and is only looked upon as an expedient for securing votes, the fact that judges can be relied upon to fine Democrats and Republi- cans alike, and to prevent the Park from lapsing into a sporting ground for roughs, is, certainly, worthy of being specially noted.

Once at the end of this avenue, we turn rapidly to the left, and find ourselves fairly in the upper park. Now that the lower division is so nearly completed—hardly any thing remaining to be done there but to finish certain architectural structures, such as the Terrace, and the separate play-houses for the boys, girls, and little children—the Commissioners are pushing on the improvements in the upper portion of the area. All over the Park, we believe, the roads and foot-paths are either completed, or in a fair way to be so, and only need to be kept in repair. All the solid work, the foundation, is done, and time, and the new needs of the hour, will develop the ornamented points. Up to this time, as appears by the last report, the eleventh, the total expenditures for the Park, from May 1st, 1857, to January 1st, 1868, have amounted to five million, one hundred and eighty thousand, two hundred and ninety-nine dollars, and eleven cents, leaving a balance in the treasury of one hundred and twenty-six thousand and seventy-six dollars and fifty-one cents. We doubt if so large a sum of money was ever more judiciously expended by any government, for the culture and enjoyment of the people, and no less are we to be congratulated on the exceptional fact, that, from first to last, the management of the Park has been so prudent, so honest, and so wise, that it has never been called in question by any persons speaking with authority. When, in 1861, a committee was appointed, at the instigation of a few malcontents—disappointed ex-commissioners and discharged officers—to examine into the affairs, condition, and progress of the Park; the report of the committee was unanimous in its approval of all that had been done, and commended the entire management of the Park to the Legislature and people of the State. It may be added that this committee was peculiarly competent to the examination it was set to make, being composed of the Hon. John McLeod Murphy, widely known as an engineer of skill and experience, the Hon. Allen Monroe, an experienced mer-

chant and banker, and the Hon. Francis M. Rotch, a vice-president
of the New York State Agricultural Society, and a well-known
agriculturist.

The portion of the Park that seems to be the least advanced
is the region lying between the northern end of the new Reservoir, Ninety-sixth Street, and the vicinity of the Museum at
Mount St. Vincent, One-Hundred-and-Second Street.   Just beyond this point, the grounds look more trim, and, as the carriage

THE MUSEUM AND RESTAURANT FROM HARLEM MEER.

stops at the museum, the visitor observes with pleasure that this
building which, not a great while ago, was a forlorn barracks,
has been made by the hand of care and taste to assume a very
agreeable appearance, a truly domestic air, to which its irregular
shape and rambling rooms are found quite conducive.   We have
called this a museum, but it is rather a large restaurant, the
museum being only that portion of the building formerly occu-

pied by the chapel of the convent. This is filled, at present, with the casts of the late Mr. Crawford's various sculptures, which were presented to the Central Park by his widow, in 1860. There are, in all, eighty-seven of these casts, consisting of statues, bas-reliefs, and sketches, and as they are arranged in this large and ample hall they present quite an imposing appearance, and prove a great attraction to multitudes of people. The sculpture-gallery can be entered directly from the house, or by an elevated gallery, roofed, but open on each side, which connects it with the opposite end of the building. From this gallery, and from the balconies of the house, a fine view is obtained of the northeastern corner of the Park, and of the city in that direction. As we eat our ices, we look down upon the lawns with their rococo beds of flowers, their fountains playing airy tricks like their neighbors of the Terrace, and, beside these, the nursery and kitchen-garden, where persons of a rural turn of mind may learn the look of vegetables when growing. Here the citizen, whose education has been neglected, may learn that cabbages do not grow upon bushes like roses, that green peas are not the fruit of a tree, and that tomatoes are not produced by nature, ready canned. Information of this kind is at once so rare and so valuable, that we cannot doubt the Commissioners have done well in appropriating this patch for its dissemination. Indeed it serves a double use, for, as the Eleventh Report assures us, " The vegetables which, while growing, serve the purpose of instruction, are used, when ripe, to feed the animals."

The Restaurant, to which the main body of this building is devoted, is one of the pleasantest places of the kind in the city or near it. There are large rooms with many tables for those who like a crowd, and there are small rooms with few tables, or only one, for those who wish to enjoy, in private, the society of their friends. Then, there are the piazzas, the balconies, and the open grounds, where creams, ices, and light refreshments can be enjoyed in the fresh air, and thus it would seem that every taste must be suited. The grass and flowers are beautiful, and well cared for, the fountains fill the air with coolness and pleasant sound, and, before long, a band equal to that in the lower

HARLEM MEER.

park will discourse as eloquent music, and divide with that, the suffrages of the crowd.

Just beyond the Restaurant-Museum the road makes a sharp double turn, keeping inside the line of the old fortifications, and skirting the edge of the Harlem Meer, yet not so closely but that a foot-path leaving the kitchen-garden has room to run to the earth-works, and to pass between it and the shore of the Meer. Having crossed the slender arm of water that connects the Loch and the Meer, by a bridge, the road keeps on, nearly straight, to the end of the Park, and, after two turn-outs for the gates at the Sixth and Seventh avenues, continues to the Eighth Avenue angle, and then begins its return to the lower park.

The body of water covering an area of nearly thirteen acres, and appropriately called the Harlem Meer, thus retaining a name connected with the early history of the island, is formed, like the

HARLEM MEER AND OLD FORTIFICATIONS WITH RESTAURANT.

Terrace Lake, by collecting the drainage of one of the valleys that cross the Park. We have already passed two of these in our drive, and this one is the third and last. The valley extends in a diagonal, quite from one side of the Park to the other, and the water collected by springs and surface drainage is made to do duty here, as in the other valleys, in ornamentation, so as to unite beauty and use. The water first appears on the western side of the Park opposite One-Hundred-and-First Street, and so near the boundary as only to admit a foot path between it and the wall; here it is spread out into a small expanse, which has been called the Pool. A small runnel connects this with another expanse, longer in shape than the Pool, and with steeper sides, to which the name of the Loch has been given, a little ambitiously, as it seems to us. But, to get names for these places, which are entirely appropriate, is by no means easy, and we are not disposed to fault-finding. Another stream, somewhat longer than the former, connects the picturesque little Loch with the large and spreading Meer, the surplus water of which is carried off by the city sewers. The eastern end of the Harlem Meer extends from One-Hundred-and-Sixth Street to within a few feet of One-Hundred-and-Tenth Street, the limit of the Park on the north. A foot-path runs round the whole water, and at two points there are small beaches. This makes, in winter, a fine skating pond, accommodating nearly as many skaters as the Terrace Lake. Owing to its greater distance from the city proper, it has not been so much frequented as the lower water, but, in time, there will be but little difference in the number of people who will seek both of them, thronging in from either end of the island. Along a portion of the southern border of the Meer the shore rises quite abruptly, and the summit is crowned by the remains of the earth-works erected during the war of 1812. These have been neatly turfed, and the surface retained, as nearly as possible, in its original shape, so that this makes a pretty station from which to survey the spreading water at our feet.

The drive in this upper portion of the Park is much more winding and irregular than in the lower part; it is particularly circuitous in the northwestern quarter, where, at times, it be-comes mildly picturesque, and has really a great deal of beauty and variety. On a rocky summit near the northern boundary still stands a stone Block-House—called so, we presume, from its rectangular shape—used either as a magazine or as a fortification, probably the latter, in the war of 1812. It made a point in the line of defences that crossed the island here, and of which abundant other traces remain at points farther west. It had become a receptacle for rubbish, but the Commissioners caused it to be cleared out, and a simple stairs put up on the inside in

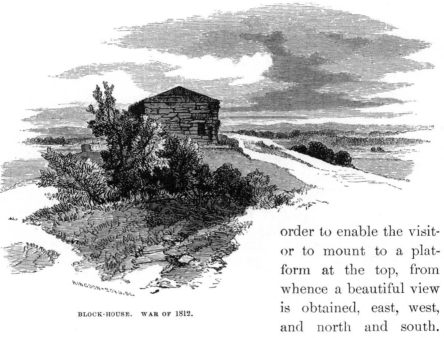

BLOCK-HOUSE.   WAR OF 1812.

order to enable the visitor to mount to a platform at the top, from whence a beautiful view is obtained, east, west, and north and south. The Hudson River and East River, with their opposite shores; the Harlem plain or flats, crossed by the new avenues and Boulevards; Mount Morris, the new square which was put under the charge of the Commissioners, and then, for no reason that can be got at, taken away from them; the slopes of the southern sides of the valley in which Manhattanville lies, and on which the much-talked-of Morning-side Park is to be laid out: on the east, the arches of the Viaduct for the New Haven Railroad, seen in our cut; then, far away to the north, the noble High Bridge, with its lofty arches plainly seen, and beyond, farther and farther, the swelling uplands of Westchester, a blue-gray mist under the noon-day sun.

In this part of the Park, the surface of the ground is strewed with large bowlders, and the rocky stratum that underlies the whole Park, and which, as we have before remarked, crops out, or did originally crop out, over almost every square foot of ground,

VIEW NEAR BLOCK-HOUSE, LOOKING EAST.

has been allowed to show itself here in considerable masses rising out of the green turf, or by the sides of the walks, with flowers encircling their base, and vines of honeysuckle, and wisteria, and the wild grape climbing all about them. The main drive encircles the tract in which the most of these rocks are found, leaving the walks among them to be enjoyed by persons on foot. In time this pretty, picturesque spot will be second in its attractions only to the Ramble; at present, the vines and shrubs have not made a sufficient growth, and the place is too far off for those who live south of the Park, but the views from it are finer now than they will be in ten years, for by that time we may look for the rising flood of the city to have swallowed up whatever there is left of grass and trees and garden ground between this and Harlem, and there will be nothing left for us to see from this height but the bricks and mortar of the city.

Within the last year a small spring has been opened in the rocky ground east of the Block-House, and its overflow has been so husbanded as to make a slender stream that runs with a musical tinkle down the slopes, falling from one rocky or reedy basin to another, until, at length, in a series of pretty miniature cascades, it reaches a circular pool on the level ground at the foot of the hill. Just at present, the surroundings of this streamlet are somewhat bare, but, in a year or two, when the water plants are fairly growing, and the climbing vines have been won to run this way, and the birds that haunt such streams have found the road hither, there will have been added to this portion of the Park all that it needed before, to make it as picturesque as the neighboring Ravine, to which it is designed to serve as an artistic balance and contrast.

A path leads down by rocky steps to the Harlem Meer, from which we turned off to look at the Block-House, and to enjoy the view from its top. Following this path, and reaching the walk that runs along the western side of the Meer, we come to the stream of which we have before spoken as draining the northernmost of the valleys that cross the Park. A light bridge crosses the stream, and the path leading on by the water side for two hundred feet or so, we come to a picturesque bridge by which the carriage-road is enabled to cross both the foot-path and the brook. It is formed of large stones piled rudely together, and forming a rather savage and dangerous looking tunnel, under which we pass for the first time with not a little inward mis-

giving, which nothing but our confidence in the skill of the
Park engineers enables us to overcome. The rocks are not
laid in mortar, but are held in place by their weight alone, and

ROCKY BRIDGE IN RAVINE.

an ample, comfortable seat of rustic wood-work enables us to get
pleasantly accustomed to the horror of the situation while we
eat our luncheon. Over all such structures as this, the art of

the Park gardener hastens to throw some veil of bloom or verdure that, in time, will take away, for timid people, the look

of danger, and will recon-
cile the artist to what
would else seem too bare
and bleak for such sur-
roundings. Already the
Cobea, a rampant and
showy climber, with its
curious purple bell-flow-

CASCADE ABOVE THE ROCKY ARCHWAY.

ers is beginning to clothe these rocks, and before long the more
hardy vines will have covered the whole archway.

Passing through the Tunnel, we come upon an extremely

pretty cascade which falls into the upper end of a spreading
pool.   A foot-path leads off from the main one upon which we
are walking, and brings us to a point where we can get a better
view of the tumbling water.   Close by is a spring welling out
of the rock, with a friendly cup suspended, and the path that
has led us to this pool will take us, if we follow it, up the opposite side of the hollow to another walk that runs, like the

CASCADE AT HEAD OF LOCH.

one we left, along the border of the Loch, but not so near its
shore.

Taking either of these paths, and they both meet again at
the head of the Loch, we get a view of this pretty piece of
water which should have a colony of wild ducks of its own to
be in keeping with its name.   It is a longish stretch of water,
with its steep sides in a way to be well wooded before many

years, and though it is calm and tranquil enough for nearly all its
length, reflecting the trees that hang about it, and the blue of
the overarching sky, while the snow-white swans, whose home
it is.

"Float double, swan and shadow."

But, toward the farther end, where it receives the water of the
running stream that flows from the Pool, the smooth surface

BRIDGE OVER THE CASCADE.

of the Loch is ruffled by the tumble of two cascades, one of
which is made by the main stream seeking a lower level, and
the other by a small runnel that flows into the Loch from the
wooded hillside at the left. The visitor should not fail to leave
the walk he has been following, at this point, and trace the
smaller of the two streams to its source, not very remote.

The path leads up the bushy slope almost at right angles
to the walk that follows the margin of the Loch, and the visitor

has hardly gone many steps beyond the first cascade before he
hears the low thunder of another, and evidently a larger one.
Pushing on, he finds himself, after a short walk, in one of the
prettiest of the many pretty nooks, of which there are so many

SABRINA'S POOL, NEAR THE RAVINE.

in the Park; yet, charming as is the place, we had passed many
a day in the Ravine, and had often sat with book or luncheon
within a few hundred feet of it, before we discovered its existence.   After once or twice crossing the stream that bubbles
so pleasantly, half hidden by the leaves, the path widens, and
we see, at the left hand, an ample seat of rustic-work, whose
cozy ins-and-outs answer to the irregularities of the large rock
against which it is placed, and which is almost entirely covered

from sight by a canopy of wild vine. Directly opposite this, the pretty cascade shown in our cut falls into a circular basin over a rocky wall, the clefts and crannies in which are set thick with mosses and branching ferns, while the side of the basin next the path is bordered with a bright circle of the flowers that love the neighborhood of water. Here, in the spring, we come to find the iris and the dog-tooth violet; and, later, the cardinal-flower lightens up the shade with its splendid bloom. The place is so removed from observation by being off the accustomed walk, that one might easily sit here for hours together, and read or sketch without seeing any other visitor, unless it were the grey rabbit, who lives hereabouts, and who sometimes comes hopping along the path; or the robin, who has built her nest in this hazle-brake, and who, if we are very quiet, will even pick up our crumbs for her children's dinner; or the dark butterflies, who hover over these beds like flowers over flowers; or, best of all, the humming-bird, who darts suddenly out of space at the rosy blossoms of this great Weigela-bush twenty times in an hour, and if he happens to find another of his family here before him, will treat us to as pretty a fight, as fierce and determined as if he and the other little ball of green and gold fire were human beings contending for a continent. With such sights we can amuse ourselves in this shaded retreat; and if it were not for the occasional rumble of a carriage over the road near at hand, we might easily forget the neighborhood of the noisy city. If we follow the path a little farther on, we come to this archway of cut-stone, which leads us under the drive that crosses the Park nearly on a line with One-Hundred-and-Second Street, connecting the two main drives running north and south on either side of the Park, and issuing upon the two bounding avenues by the "Girls'" and "Boys'" gates. This archway is very low, and by no means cheerful; but its want of height gives it a quaint look that is in keeping with the surrounding objects. For this nook has an aspect different from any thing else in the Park, and pleases by its unexpectedness as well as by its picturesqueness. The darkness of the archway too makes the sunlighted landscape seen from either end more bright; we look out upon the world as from a cavern. And, in time, it will be still more like a cavern, for it is fast being overgrown with the trailing vines planted above its mouth, and the trees and shrubs overhead, and about its sides, already conceal a large part of the stone-work. On entering the archway

ARCH OVER FOOT-PATH NEAR RAVINE.

we hardly lose the sound of the first cascade before we hear the rumbling of a second, and presently come upon it at the farther end of the tunnel, on the left hand side of the entrance. This cascade falls over rocks into a rocky basin, and is at present less attractive than the one at the other end, because the vines and shrubs and water-plants, the ferns and mosses, have not had time to grow, and soften the rude outlines of the stones. The water from this basin, after passing under the foot-path, and also under the bridle-path and carriage-drive, reissues at the northern end of the tunnel, and, falling over the bank, makes the cascade before which we sat so long, watching the butterflies and humming-birds. The way in which this liquid problem is solved, does not, at first, appear to the uninitiated, to whom the two cascades appear to fall from nearly the same level, and many will find it far more interesting and instructive to spend a lazy hour in making out how the ingenious engineers have contrived this

BRIDGE FOR CARRIAGE-ROAD OVER RAVINE.

puzzle, than in feeding rabbits and robins, or following the victories of quarrelsome humming-birds.

As this path, if followed farther, will only lead us away from the Ravine, and as there are no objects of peculiar interest in this neighborhood beyond the dell with its twin cascades, we will retrace our steps, and seek again the head of the Loch. The foot-path, after passing a turn-out leading over the rustic bridge which spans the small cascade, of which we gave a picture on page

178, continues by the side of a narrow runnel connecting the Loch with the much larger Pool. Near the upper end of this runnel, and just before it widens into the Pool, we come to a singular bridge crossing both the foot-path and the water, a combination of rustic wood-work and stone-masonry that seems to us by no means in good taste. It is ugly in its design, the lines being neither beautiful nor strong; and, although we have no doubt it is thoroughly well built, and capable of bearing all the pressure that it will ever be called upon to bear, it does not look strong, and this apparent weakness is fatal to any claims that may be made for it on the score of design. As the abutments are very solid, we hope the Commissioners will before long throw an arch of stone over this foot-path, and the stream of water that runs beside it. Apart from any question of taste, this bridge is an object of considerable curiosity. On the left hand side of the foot-path, in a recess of the abutment of the bridge, is a large and comfortable seat made of cedar branches and twigs, from which the bark has been removed, and in the opposite abutment an ample arched recess contains a huge boulder, whose smooth face is kept continually black and moist with the drip of water from springs in the bank above. Water-loving plants are gradually making a lodgment in the clefts and crannies of this rough masonry, and it is likely that before long the whole interior of the archway will be transformed into a cool green grotto, a place into which the summer heats will be afraid to come, for fear of taking cold.

It is pretty, too, sitting on this comfortable sofa, to look out upon the waterfall that, in a succession of plunges from the higher waters of the Pool, gains the seclusion of the basin on the other side of the archway. When an abundance of rain has fallen, and the Pool is full, this fall is perhaps the finest in the Park, but it is rarely too low to be unattractive. Indeed, the natural drainage of the ground, with the husbanding of the springs, secures to all the waterfalls, as to all the sheets of water, large and small, throughout the Park, an abundant supply even in seasons of drought.

By crossing the bridge that spans this cascade, we can continue our walk on the other side of the Pool, or we can keep to that on which we began, if we prefer. A glance at the map will show

RUSTIC BRIDGE AND CASCADE IN RAVINE.

that the walks are so arranged as to permit the visitor to make the circuit of all the three pieces of water, the Pool, the Loch, and the Meer, which drain this northernmost of the transverse valleys of the Park. Not that the path continually keeps to the very border of the water; sometimes it leads us to a considerable distance from it, but rarely so far that we are not in sight of it, and, even then, only for a moment.   Nor are we ever long without coming to one of the six bridges that enable us to cross from one side to the other, and thus perpetually to vary our walk.   It must be remembered, too, that at the time we are writing the whole northern half of the Park is far from being finished, and that every year, for some years to come, the Commissioners will be adding to the attractions and to the variety of this neighborhood.

THE POOL.

Naturally, it is a region much more capable of picturesque treatment than the lower park, or than that portion of the upper park that lies near the Great Reservoir.   In the northwestern quarter, for example, there is a profusion of scattered boulders beside a great quantity of fixed rock, and this gives opportunity to the Commissioners to open new paths, almost every season, in and out between these clefts and among these craggy irregularities.

Such a walk has been opened, since the tenth report was issued, across the space thickly strewn with boulders, which lies along the western end of the Meer and the stream that connects it with the Loch. It is an extremely pretty rural path, and resembles some of those we find in the Ramble, except that it is much wilder.

The Pool is a larger sheet of water than the Loch, and much more irregular in its shape. A large house, probably occupied

ON THE POOL LOOKING NORTHWEST.

by some of the people employed in the Park, stands at some distance from it, but on rising ground, so that it is easily seen from the walk at frequent points. Indeed, it appears much nearer to the Pool than the map shows it to be, and the northern side of the Lake looks, in places, like the lawn stretching down from the house to the water. There is a small rocky island in one place, and portions of the shore are somewhat rocky, while at the eastern end there is a miniature beach, where one may always be pretty sure of finding the ducks and some queer geese or other, oiling their plumage for another plunge into this water, of which they have the monopoly, as against all the little boys in the world longing to emulate them in swimming. The paths on either side the Pool are united by a cross path at the western end, and are both led to the "Boys' Gate," opposite One Hundredth Street.

OLD HOUSE BY RESERVOIR.

Another walk, however, leads us farther south, and enables us to continue our ramble within the limits of the Park.

The road now runs on the western side of the Park, skirting the wide tract of open ground called the Meadows, then crossing the fourth traffic-road for the second time, and winding in and out among the thickly planted trees of the open space between the old Reservoir and the Eighth Avenue. This portion of the road the Commissioners intend for a winter drive, and they have accordingly planted a great number of evergreens on either side, not monotonously, but with plenty of agreeable, open space, clustering them thickest on the land that slopes from the Reservoir. Near the Reservoir, in the northeast corner of this parallelogram, formerly stood an old house of considerable size, surrounded by large willows. This has lately been removed, the Croton Aqueduct Board, which owned it and used it as a dwelling for some of the persons employed in its service in connection with the two Reservoirs, having erected a new dwelling-house of stone on the ground between the old Reservoir and

SLEIGHING BY THE WILLOWS.

the fourth traffic-road. The old willows that surrounded the former house have been allowed to stand, and, with their irregular forms and drooping foliage, make a picturesque contrast with the evergreens that surround them.

The portions of the Park on either side of the old Reservoir are arranged with a good deal of skill, to make that structure as little of an eye-sore as possible, but the treatment of the western

side is at present far more effective, both in itself and for the end
proposed, than that of the eastern.   But, with skilful planting, the
two sides will no doubt before long become very nearly equal,
though it will hardly ever be possible to make the existence of
the Reservoir forgotten altogether.   The plan shows that the space
on the west is much more cut up with walks and drives than the
eastern; the carriage-ride and the horse-path run quite apart, and
the foot-paths are almost as winding here as in the Ramble near by.

BALCONY BRIDGE, WEST SIDE.

As the drive passes
along the western side of
the Lake, it crosses the
Balcony Bridge, of which
we spoke in our earlier
pages, while to the right
hand, between this bridge and the Eighth Avenue, the foot-path
crosses the pretty rustic bridge seen in our cut, and just before
reaching the Balcony Bridge, the foot-path at the left crosses the
elegant bridge of oak and iron, and enters the Ramble near the
Cave.

Southwest of the Lake, the drive, after dividing and passing
round the oblong piece of ground on which the Restaurant for gentlemen more particularly is to be erected, unites again to divide
immediately, and turns to left and right.   The road to the right

keeps on in a line as direct as may be, first sweeping gently into a point where it crosses the first traffic-road, in common with the horse-path and two foot-paths, so that the traffic-road is not seen at all, and the four roads are hid from each other by shrubbery. From this point the road trends slightly outward, crossing the horse-path once, and, a little farther on, the foot-path, by bridges, and soon reaches the Merchants' Gate, at the southwestern angle of the Park, Fifty-ninth Street and Eighth Avenue.

RUSTIC BRIDGE, NEAR BALCONY BRIDGE, LOOKING WEST.

The turn to the left, at the point we just started from, is a more interesting way of leaving the Park. It strikes at once for the middle of the Park, runs along nearly parallel to the Mall, though not in a straight line, and at its southern end gives the visitor the choice of passing in to the East Drive, and so out by the Fifth Avenue; or, by keeping due south, and then turning west, to reach the Eighth Avenue gate.

In the very beginning of the seventeenth century, Lord Bacon wrote in his Advancement of Learning:—"In preparation of medicines, I do find strange, especially considering how mineral medicines have been extolled, and that they are safer for the outward than inward parts, that no man hath sought to make an imitation by art of natural baths and medicinable fountains:" and he counts such methods of cure among the things in which our knowledge

RUSTIC BRIDGE, NEAR BALCONY BRIDGE, LOOKING EAST.

is deficient. But the reader of these pages does not need to be told that this want has long been supplied, and that he may drink in his own house, or at more than one counter, to-day, a perfect imitation of any one of the notable mineral springs either of this country or of Europe. A firm in our city have obtained permission from the Board to erect in the Park a building for the sale of these mineral waters, and we shall find it nearly completed on the road we are now following, west of the Terrace and on a rising ground. The building is to be a very elegant one; it was designed by the Messrs. Vaux and Withers, and will cost $30,000.

As we pass the Mall, especially if it happen to be on a music-day, the contrast between the views on either side is quite striking.

OAK BRIDGE.

On our left hand, if we are leaving the Park, the long walk, with its crowds of gayly-dressed people clustered thick as bees about the graceful flower-like music stand, makes a bright and cheerful picture, suggestive of the city and of city life; while on the right is the broad, lawn-like expanse of the green, with its flock of one

hundred and sixty-three Southdown sheep, with their keeper, presenting an appearance of pastoral simplicity as he wanders, crook

in hand, after his
nibbling charge, and
carrying the mind far
enough away from
the sights and sounds
of the environing

OAK BRIDGE, SECOND VIEW.

city.   If we are of a too practical turn to let this pretty scene
lead us in imagination to those

> "Russet lawns and fallows grey,
>   Where the nibbling flocks do stray,
> *   *   *   *   *
>   Meadows trim. with daisies pied,
>   Shallow brooks and rivers wide,"

that are to be found in the true country, we may please ourselves
with the prudent reflection that these sheep make most excellent

mutton, and produce the best of wool, so that their utility fairly balances their good looks; beside which, they keep the lawn in the best condition by constant cropping and manuring.

THE SHEPHERD.

As we cross the traffic-road, we come in sight of the Play-Ground, an open tract of ten acres, exclusively devoted to boys' games. The Controller and Treasurer of the Park, Mr. Andrew

H. Green, to whose watchful eye and constant supervision we are indebted, and not less to his ingenious suggestions, for much that makes the Park attractive to the masses of the people, has always strongly sympathized with Messrs. Vaux and Olmsted in their desire to make the Park a place of popular education as well as one of mere enjoyment. At the same time, it has been evident that, considering the limits of the Park, and the great variety of tastes to be consulted, it cannot be conceded that the lawns and open spaces of the city's only pleasure-ground shall be open at all times freely to those who wish to use them for athletic games. Nothing

PLAY-GROUND.

is more easily injured than fine turf—nothing harder to keep in repair. And there are many who do not see why it should be used and treated so carefully. They do not agree with Bacon, who says:—"Nothing is more Pleasant to the Eye than Greene Grasse kept finely shorne," but think it is intended solely to walk or romp upon. To permit any number of people, whether it were the majority or the minority, to deal with the chief ornament of a pleasure-ground, in which both the majority and the minority have equal rights, is plainly impossible, and how to manage the matter without injury to the Park, and yet with due concession to the popular feeling, has been a difficult problem.

But, at last, it has been settled this way: On certain days, music days or general holidays, the public is allowed free use of particular pieces of grass or lawn for walking, and for the little children to play upon. It may be said here that the damage done to the grass on all such occasions always takes several days to repair! Beside this particular permission, the ten-acre tract, along which we are just now driving, has been set apart as a boys' play-ground, and it is used three days in each week by such boys attending the public or the larger private schools as are thought by their teachers to have earned the privilege by good conduct. This is a reward of merit that the boys appreciate, and it has thus far proved a great incentive to study and to good conduct. Thousands of our schoolboys have used the Play-Ground on these terms since Mr. Green first established the system. Nor are the girls to be forgotten. They are to have a play-ground of their own south of the Children's Gate, near the Fifth Avenue and Seventy-second Street, and a pretty house has been erected for their accommodation, where they may make simple changes in their dress, lay aside hats and cloaks, overshoes and umbrellas, and where they may find croquet balls, rings, and mallets, hoops, skipping-ropes, and even bats and balls, if they have got as far.

The increased demands upon the area of the Play Ground by the boys of the public schools, have made it necessary to have a building for their accommodation also, at a point near their place of play. The foundations of an extremely simple, but very pretty, house of brick and stone have been laid at the north end of the Play-Ground, to serve as a place of deposit and distribution of the bats and balls and other paraphernalia of the game of base-ball, and also for toilet arrangements. The capacity of the Play-Ground is often found insufficient to accommodate all who come to play. When the bases, into which the ground is divided, are filled, as is often the case, arrangements are made for the rest on the neighboring Green. The Commissioners of the Park are thus

developing, year after year, their intention to make the Park useful
to the children of the city, and an aid in its beneficent system of
common-school education.   The whole Park is looked upon by
them as an adjunct to that system—a necessary and logical part
of it.

The mention of the Children's Gate reminds us that we have
made no allusion as yet to the names that have been given to the
Park entrances by the Commissioners, and which it is intended, at
some future day, to associate, by some simple but expressive symbolism, with the gate-ways that will be erected at these points.

VIEW NEAR BOYS' GATE, LOOKING WEST.

The naming of the gates early received the attention of the
Commission, and, in the Fifth Annual Report (1862), there was
published a lengthy "Report on the Nomenclature of the Gates
of the Park," the suggestions in which were adopted by the Commissioners, and have since been carried out with scarcely any
modifications.

There can hardly be any doubt, we should think, as to the
desirableness of having names given to the several gate-ways by
authority, and that, too, as early as possible, so as to prevent
what, for lack of a better term, we may call nick-names being
fastened upon the entrances by the public, as has often happened

in the older countries. Beside, there is a certain unity of thought and design in the Park itself, and it seems fitting enough that the naming of the entrances should grow out of that theory which the Commissioners have been aiming to carry out in the arrangement and regulation of the Park ever since the work was fairly begun. The Central Park is the pleasure-ground of the chief city in a great republic. It has not been set apart by any privileged class for its own use and entertainment, but is the creation of the whole people of the City of New York for their own enjoyment, and, with a large hospitality, they invite the rest of the world to share it freely with them on equal terms. In naming the gates, therefore, that are to give entrance to the grounds thus set apart from trade and traffic and mere material use, for purposes of elevated pleasure and education in higher things, it has been thought fittest to select such names as will make every working member of the community, whether he work with his head or his hands, feel his personal ownership in the Park. To carry out this idea, which is not the less generous for being strictly true, has not been easy, nor, perhaps, have the Commissioners wholly succeeded, but their selection of names leaves little to be desired, and is to be commended as both sensible and appropriate. Every one of them admits of interesting sculpture and striking symbolism upon the gateway that will be built for it in the future; nor is it by any means impossible that the several trades, professions, and classes of men represented by these names may be moved themselves to erect, or, at any rate, to ornament, the gate-ways that belong to them with the statues of their famous members, or with symbolic decorations of such elegance or richness as they can afford.

The original report supplied names for twenty gates,* and

---

* These were as follows:—The Artisan, The Artist, The Merchant, The Scholar, The Cultivator, The Warrior, The Mariner, The Engineer, The Hunter, The Fisherman, The Woodman, The Miner, The Explorer. The Inventor, The Foreigner, The

it is more than likely that in time this number of entrances will be needed, but at present there are not so many. Although the report was printed, as we have said, in 1862, and ordered to be accepted in the same year, it was not until 1865 that its suggestions would seem to have been formally adopted by the Commissioners. The convenient "Park Guide" with the accompanying "Reference," which now appears regularly in the annual reports, was first contained in that for 1864; in it the names of the gates are printed in the "Reference," but are not engraved upon the map itself. In this list of 1864 there were only sixteen names of gates given, instead of the twenty originally proposed. The Fisherman, The Inventor, and The Explorer are omitted, and the Engineer and Miner are both included in one. We observe, too, that the name "Stranger" has been adopted in preference to Foreigner, where the report suggests either, and that "Farmer" has been preferred to "Cultivator," probably as being more familiar. In the next report, that for 1865, we find the arrangement adopted which has since continued in force. There are now eighteen gates instead of sixteen; the names of the Fisherman and the Inventor are still omitted, the Engineers' and the Miners' gates are again separated as was at first proposed, and the Explorer of the original report is restored, under the name of The Pioneer, a change for the better, since, while it does honor to all such men as Columbus and Hudson, it also includes the pioneer of our western country, and the brave fellows who have scaled the Rocky Mountains and laid the foundations of a new empire for us on the Pacific shore.

Of course, if it is found desirable or necessary, new gates can be added at any time, and in case the number should be increased to the original twenty, the names "Fisherman" and "Inventor" well deserve to be given to the new ones. The

Boys, The Girls, The Women, The Children, and All Saints.—Report for 1862, page 135.

Fishermen, no less than the Hunters, are a race apart, and the craft has played a more conspicuous part in the history of our relations with foreign powers. We have been ready to go to war two or three times for their rights, and are quite ready to go to war for them whenever it shall be necessary. Socially, too, they are a very important class, as many villages, and even large towns are almost entirely made up of fishermen's families, and, what is more, their craft is not merely a temporary pursuit, disappearing before civilization like that of the hunter, but a steady business, as well recognized as that of the farmer, and while quite as ancient as his, likely to last as long. So, by all means, let us have a gate for the Fisherman: it will be easy to decorate it.

The Inventor, too, ought to be honored, especially here in America, where he has played such a notable part. What with statues of Franklin, Fulton, Morse, Hoe, Whitney, Howe, and Morton, the gate would be a trophy more splendid than could be raised by any other country to her own citizens as benefactors of the whole world.

As we leave the Park by whichever road, we catch glimpses of pretty, rural scenery between the clustering trees. We look across the broad Play-Ground with its delightful sweeps of verdant lawn unbroken by the smallest shrub or tree, to where, on the opposite side there rises above the thick enclosing wall of foliage, the rocky knoll from which the spectator can watch a dozen games of base-ball at once, if he have Cæsar's power of divided concentration. And what a scene it is on this sunbright October day, with its merry, noisy, hubbub crowd of young barbarians all at play, and the gay girdle of their smiling friends and sisters looking on at this essentially American tournament! Is there a pleasanter sight on earth than to see a gathering of boys like this, every one of whom has earned his right to his afternoon's sport by good conduct and diligence in school, neither letting his full obedience to duty and his thorough performance of his task quell his animal spirits, nor his inborn love of play get the mastery over his ambition. Such a sight as this makes the heart hopeful, it is one of the bright sides of our American life, which has its dark sides, as we all know, but even a poet like Gray might have looked on this bright spectacle without the gloomy foreboding that saddens his famous Ode.

The new house that has just been finished for the accommodation of the little children, near their Play-Ground, is not so ornamental a structure as the Boys' House, but it is an exceedingly cozy, comfortable nest, and tempts one to inquire within for permanent lodgings. Here the little ones, with their nurses or sisters, can take shelter from a sudden shower, or procure some light refreshment suited to their tender years. Near this pretty cottage, too, the Alderney cows are to be tethered, as in some of the foreign parks, and will supply an abundance of milk, whose origin will be above suspicion, as its excellence is pretty sure to be above compare. Whether city people will like it is another matter; of course those who have been brought up on milkman's milk will not recognize the taste of nature's product, and may pronounce it insipid, but if fashion should once take a liking to it, woe to the luckless milkmen! Their occupation would be gone.

In spite of the near neighborhood of the city, which cannot be completely shut out by any thing but a very lofty growth of trees, we are sometimes surprised, even in this southernmost portion of the Park, by a view like that which one gets by keeping on in a direction east of the Children's Shelter and looking down upon the Pond. We have already given several views of this pretty water, but they are all very different from this, which, except at one point, and that not impossible to be planted out in time, has a quiet beauty that strikes one the more pleasantly from the surprise of finding it so near the most noisy entrance of the Park. And near the gate-way at the Seventh Avenue, if we are on horseback, we pass under the graceful iron arch-way, whose lines are almost hid by the thick veil of American Ivy that runs rampant over it. The walk it

VIEW NEAR THE POND—FIFTY-NINTH STREET.

carries runs along the side of the Play-Ground, and leads us directly to the Mall through the Marble Arch.

We sometimes hear disparaging remarks aimed at the Central Park because it is inferior in size to a few of the great parks of the world. But, for ourselves, our pride in it has never been in its size, nor, indeed, in any thing that has as yet been put in it by way of ornament. We are proud of it because it is the first undertaking of the kind in our own country, and because its entire management, from the first day until now, has been such as to recommend enterprises of this nature to the whole country. In no other city in the world is there a park better cared for or managed with greater skill and efficiency than our own. When we are brought to shame by the vile and dishonest government of the City of New York, and reproached with that dishonor as if it were an argument against Republicanism, we point to the perfect order and quiet of the Central Park as a proof that we have the remedy in our hands when we choose to apply it.

Little now remains to say, but as we near the Artists' Gate we see troops upon troops of merry children with their nurses, coming in from the cars, laughing, chatting, crowing, all on their way to the Children's Shelter and the Children's Play-Ground. This is a new institution in the Park, and it ought to be called the Mothers' Blessing, for surely it is a pleasant spot to fly to out of the dust and heat of the city. Here under this ample shelter with its fragrance of cedar and cool withdrawal from the sun, the little ones may play all day without the possibility of danger, or may, even, sleep, with mother or nurse to watch them, on these ample benches. Here are a multitude of rustic tables of various sizes for smaller or larger parties, where the simple luncheon may be eaten, and in time sleek-coated cows upon the lawn will give the purest, sweetest milk to this bevy of little ones. It was a happy thought to provide so generously and beautifully for the youngest children, and who can tell what a difference it may make in the health and beauty of the coming generations, the having such a place and opportunities for play and exercise. The frequent contact with grass and flowers and trees, the mere seeing of the sky, is something bracing and health-giving, and the Park might well have been made for this alone.

And so we leave the Park with mingled feelings of pride and thankfulness, promising ourselves many pleasant days in

its cheerful sun-light, becoming better and better acquainted with all that is beau-tiful in it, and learning better and better to

CHILDREN'S SHELTER, SOUTHWEST OF MALL, FROM LOWER LAKE LOOKING EAST.

profit by all the wise care and trained thought that have made it what it is. But we who are in middle life can never know all its beauty. That is reserved for those for whom we have planted these shrubs and trees, and spread these level lawns.

These trees will arch over many happy generations, and thousands
who are not yet born, will enjoy the sweet green of the grass; the
wood flowers will have learned to bloom amid the hum of the city
as regularly and as profusely as in their wilding native places,
when those who made this great bequest shall have long passed
on to other scenes.   But, if it be pleasant to man to know that

THE OVAL BRIDGE NEAR SEVENTH AVENUE.

he will not be wholly forgotten, let those who conceived the
idea of this pleasure-ground, those who designed its beauties,
and those whose public spirit and untired zeal have brought it
to perfection, be sure that their memory will not pass away, but
will renew itself year by year with the waving trees and blos-
soming flowers.

"Lord, keep their memory green!"

ABOUT THE AUTHORS

Clarence C. Cook (1828–1900) was a prominent American author and art critic. Born in Dorchester, Massachusetts, Cook graduated from Harvard in 1849 and settled in New York City. His other titles include *The House Beautiful: Essays on Beds and Tables, Stools and Candlesticks* and *Art and Artists of Our Time*.

Maureen Meister has published extensively on American art and architecture of the nineteenth and early twentieth centuries. Her most recent book is *Arts and Crafts Architecture: History and Heritage in New England*, released in 2014. She holds a doctorate from Brown University and has taught at Boston area universities including Tufts, Lesley, and Northeastern.